Know Your Dog's Tru

T0267533

"I love this book! Elizabeth Johnson's knowledge of Traditional Chinese Medicine, her warmth as a healer, and her passion for dogs have come together in a true trifecta. This is not only a fun and contemplative read, it is a reference book that should be on every dog lover's shelf. Her guidance through the elements as well as the element-specific stories help you to truly see your own dogs and yourself! I also applied this to my horses and cats! I love the organization of this book. And of course, I love the attention brought to the shelter/rescue animals that need understanding right out of the gate. Bravo, Elizabeth! Well done!"

— JOAN RANQUET, animal communicator, founder of Communication
with All Life University and the Shelter Initiative, and author of
Emotional Freedom Technique for Animals and Their Humans

"*Know Your Dog's True Nature* is a fascinating and comprehensive book detailing the ancient theories of the Five Elements and how they show up within our beloved canine friends. This is a one-of-a-kind, complete guide that will enhance your relationship with your dog through the understanding of their unique and natural rhythms. As you recognize the element's characteristics and traits in your dog, be prepared to learn more about yourself as well! This wonderful book provides tangible information to identify and understand your animal's emotional and physical needs as they navigate the seasons of their life. Elizabeth Johnson has beautifully created a much-needed resource that is sure to become your go-to book for your animal's wellness journey!"

— TAMMY BILLUPS, holistic healer, interface therapist, and author of
Animal Soul Contracts and *Animal Wayshowers*

"What a fabulous book for dogs and their 2-leggeds! Elizabeth Anne Johnson's deep rapport with dogs and humans, coupled with her all-encompassing wisdom of the Five Elements of Chinese Medicine, come alive in this practical guide to recognizing and loving your dog's traits."

— CHERYL SCHWARTZ, DVM, author of *Four Paws, Five Directions:
A Guide to Chinese Medicine for Cats & Dogs*

"What frames our view will also frame our understanding. Elizabeth Anne Johnson provides us with a powerful framework for seeing our dogs in nuanced and supportive ways. The Traditional Chinese Medicine (TCM) approach of Five Element Theory takes on new life in Johnson's capable hands as she applies this ancient understanding to our dogs. *Know Your Dog's True Nature* provides a new framework for seeing and responding to our dogs and dog friends in their golden years. When we know more, when we see in new ways, we discover new options. Johnson's lifetime of experience with dogs and animals of every kind shines through, as does her compassion and healing approach to the journey we share with other species. Highly recommended!"

— SUZANNE CLOTHIER, creator of Relationship Centered Dog Training
and author of *Bones Would Rain from the Sky*

"Elizabeth's book shows you simple, understandable ways to use the Five Element techniques for better health and understanding for both your dogs and yourself. If you are interested in dogs and Traditional Chinese Medicine, this is a must-read!"

— JEFF GROGNET, DVM, veterinarian and educator at
New Earth Vet, holistic animal health courses

"This book is super fun, practical, and lively! It's a true fusion of the wisdom and healing techniques from the TCM system and an enlightened approach for any dog parent to enhance their training program."

— JESSE STERNBERG, founder of the Peaceful Alpha Project and
author of *Enlightened Dog Training*

"I have live-captured and rescued more than 150 dogs from extremely stressful situations caused by natural disasters, highway accidents, or adoption events. Elizabeth's Five-Element behavioral theories are offering me an opportunity to understand why individual dogs make individual decisions. Understanding why these "Lost Dog Syndrome" dogs behaved uniquely in the past will help me be a better dog rescuer in the future!"

— DAVE PAULI, master humane society international animal rescuer,
master dog trapper, and certified master naturalist

KNOW YOUR DOG'S TRUE NATURE

Understanding Canine Personality through the **Five Elements**

Elizabeth Anne Johnson

FINDHORN PRESS

Findhorn Press
One Park Street
Rochester, Vermont 05767
www.findhornpress.com

Text stock is SFI certified

Findhorn Press is a division of Inner Traditions International

Disclaimer

The information in this book is given in good faith and intended for information only.
Neither author nor publisher can be held liable by any person for any loss or damage
whatsoever which may arise directly or indirectly from the use of this book or any of the
information therein.

Cataloging-in-Publication data for this title is available from the Library of Congress

ISBN 979-8-88850-064-4 (print)
ISBN 979-8-88850-065-1 (ebook)

Printed and bound in the United States by Lake Book Manufacturing, Inc.
The text stock is SFI certified. The Sustainable Forestry Initiative® program promotes
sustainable forest management.

10 9 8 7 6 5 4 3 2 1

Edited by Jane Ellen Combelic
Illustrations by Elizabeth Anne Johnson, except for p. 38 (Karen Agate); pp. 165,
171 (Depositphotos); pp. 43/173 (GlobalIP/Istockphoto) pp. 15, 22, 41, 97/177,
111, 59 (Freepik); cover (getty-images-TOX5COdKWSE-unsplash).
Text design and layout by Damian Keenan
This book was typeset in Adobe Garamond Pro and Congenial Medium with
ITC Century Std used as a display typeface.

To send correspondence to the author of this book, mail a first-class letter to the
author c/o Inner Traditions • Bear & Company, One Park Street, Rochester,
VT 05767, USA and we will forward the communication, or contact the author
directly at **www.elizabethannejohnson.com**.

*Many blessings of gratitude to the thousands
of animals who helped me understand the
wild spirit within myself, uncover the deep
expansive love in my heart, and taught me
how to sing and dance like a wolf*

*and to Mark, my hero, my guardian,
my support, the one who truly understands
the medicine of the wild ones*

Contents

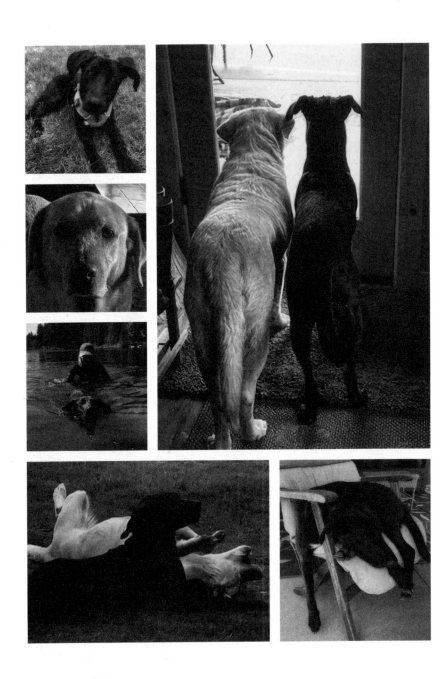

WILBUR & PRETZEL

TWO HAPPY DOGS AND THEIR ADVENTURES...

Foreword

by Allen Schoen, DVM

The life journeys Elizabeth and I have taken are like two inter-twining strands of DNA—connected by creatures, old friends, and colleagues. Now, we connect again with *Know Your Dog's True Nature* and our mutual lifelong love of animals.

It is with immense joy and honor that I write this foreword that introduces you, a dog-loving reader, to the magic of Elizabeth's wisdom and vast knowledge of the Five Element personalities of dogs.

As the world has been churning faster and more chaotically over the years from 2020 to 2024, insights and suggestions on caring for our dogs in new ways seem to be needed more than ever. In this easy-to-follow book, Elizabeth explains how to become aware of and care for the different dog personalities. The Five Element lens will help you learn about your dog and yourself while creating a gentle understanding and trust within your relationship—a trust we all strive for with our animals.

These changing times nudge us to view our relationship with our dogs in unique ways. This book will help you do that. I was introduced to the Five Element description of dog personalities when I was teaching veterinary acupuncture. In this book, Elizabeth has taken it to a higher, yet more practical, level. She makes it easy for you to understand and integrate new ways of being and doing with your dog, while having fun figuring out their behaviors and discovering their uniqueness.

Here you will learn simple observational skills to decipher the five unique patterns of the Five Element Dog Archetypes. After reading it, you may take a deep sigh of relief, and say to yourself, "Oh, that is why my dog is doing that!" In addition to appreciating the reasons why your dog is behaving a certain way, Elizabeth offers practical ways to resolve various situations based on her years of experience incorporating many approaches to different issues. Her simple solutions will help provide needed balance and harmony to your lives together. This cooperative healing message can change our world in so many ways.

In the shifting tides of this time, I find that it is essential for us to develop new ways of listening to our heart's inner guidance, and respond to the outer world with a more open mind.

Know Your Dog's True Nature can offer you a guide to new ways of walking together, hand in paw, with greater compassion for all.

ALLEN SCHOEN, DVM, MS, Ph.D. (hon.), CVA, is a pioneer in Integrated Veterinary Medicine, a professor, and an author. He also created C.A.L.M. (Conscious Animal Lovers Movement). For more information and online courses see: **www.drschoen.com**

PART 1
Introduction

1. A Dog's Eye View

If we could see with a dog's eye view, listen with their
intuitive wisdom, and speak with their humor and instinct,
the world would be a Shangrrrr-la indeed.
— MARI GAYATRI STEIN

For centuries, we humans have tried to understand and deepen our relationships with our original best friends, dogs. These furry creatures that eat, travel, protect, work, snuggle, wiggle, wag, and share life, home, and pure love with us still hold a sense of mystery. Today more than ever, with over 470 million dogs as pets in the world, there is still a heartfelt quest to simply understand our furry family members. We humans want to know: why do dogs do what they do?

Do you sometimes wish you had superhero "x-ray vision" to see into the deep recesses of your dog's behavior and personality?

Learning the ancient art of the five elements *is* like having "x-ray vision" into your dog's personality. The five elements explain the five distinct archetypal patterns of behavior we may see in our dogs, other animals, humans, and ourselves. This interspecies "x-ray vision" gives us a clear understanding of these five personality types, which can help us develop patience, empathy, and compassion within our dog/human relationships. It's a fun and easy way to create harmony with our dogs and in our heart, home, and life with others.

All animals, especially our dogs, are wisdom keepers. Dogs can help us see and feel things that we might not otherwise be aware of. They act as our teachers and guides. When we quietly observe them through the Five Element lens we see the patterns and teachings of each archetypal element. This gives us great practice for learning how to bring the Five Element theory into our human experience.

Do you truly know what your dog's wants and needs are? Do you understand those quirky behaviors that pop up occasionally and never really change?

Maybe you see consistent wonderful traits like strength and leadership, a need to be social and adored, innate nurturing and kindness, a purposeful life, or deep, flowing wisdom. But you don't know what these shiny gems mean in the big picture of your dog's life.

And when your dog suddenly changes behavior and you see irritation, nervousness, obsessiveness, aloofness, or visceral fear, are you surprised or worried?

All these traits are part of the ever-shifting balance of the ancient healing art of the Five Element theory of traditional Chinese medicine.

The Five Element theory is a mindful guidance system for finding harmony, balance, empathy, and compassion. Just by observation we can learn to understand the dynamics of our animals, ourselves, and others, and create the best version of ourselves and our dogs.

The five elements—Wood, Fire, Earth, Metal, and Water—are part of a nature-centered, ever-flowing, five-thousand-year-old modality of assessment and healing, which ultimately strives for balance. It would be challenging to teach you the entire healing art in this one book. However, *Know Your Dog's True Nature* extracts the fun part of the Five Element theory—the personality. This will help you understand the "why's?" of your dog's behavior while learning how to navigate challenges.

Extracting the Five Element personality piece from this complex healing structure, creates a profound awareness and understanding of how personality dictates how our dogs, ourselves, and others deal with stress and daily life. We know stress can have tremendous effects on our health, well-being, and balance. And, so it is with our dogs too.

When you experience life in this neutral space of Five Element observation, you are able to work with tricky situations with your dogs and others with a more open mind and heart. Thanks to the elemental understanding of who and what you are dealing with, you can guide the situation instead of reacting to it.

This book will teach you simple and distinct observation skills for the five unique patterns of the Five Element dog archetypes. Through informative chapters, tables, and real-life stories for each element, you will clearly see how each dog archetype reacts under stress. You will learn what creates stress for each dog element, as well as simple stress balancers and lifestyle measures. You will also see their individual strengths, their wants and needs, and what makes each element happy. You will learn how to support and balance these characteristics in each of the five elements, and in your relationship with your dog.

As we learn about our dog's element, we will see shades of these archetypes in ourselves and possibly in other humans. While this book is written from a dog-centered perspective, it also includes human Five Element personality and behavior descriptions that closely resemble each elemental dog description. First, we learn about our dogs, then we learn about ourselves and, to come full circle, we learn about our relationships. Our dogs as archetypal teachers give us a gentle way to enter into "who am I?"

Learning your own Five Element personality is often a profoundly honest experience that paves the way for weaving and blending the dog's elemental personality and wants and needs, with your elemental personality, wants, and needs. These perspectives will help you understand how both you and your dog deal with change, stress, relationship dynamics, and even aging.

This book guides you to a new way of being and doing, a new way of walking in the world around you with grace, vision, and knowing. It will help nurture understanding when you are searching for answers with relationship and behavioral issues with both your pets and other humans.

Ancient Minds and Methods

The five elements—Wood, Fire, Earth, Metal, and Water—are based on the universal, nature-centric premise of movement, change, and balance. In nature, as in life, nothing is static. There is ever-present creation, birth, growth, control, death, and rebirth. We see this broadly in the change of seasons, the wind, the mountains, the flow of rivers, our own bodies and minds, and a whole galaxy of other ways. Traditional Chinese medicine's Five Element theory is based on these everchanging dynamics and inter-relationships. As with nature, the Five Element theory has one persistent and ultimate goal—to create balance. My mantra has long been: Life is good, balance is better.

The overall Five Element theory is based on an ancient traditional system of seasonal "affiliations" or connections that were used to assess and treat animals and humans. To effectively assess personality, we look at the following traits: archetypes, emotions, wants, needs, stressors, balancers, and potential strengths and weaknesses for each element. This helps us see why and how each dog and human element responds to the world around them.

Each element chapter has tips for creating balance within each dog element, including our rescue and senior dogs, and offers helpful life lessons that each dog element teaches us from the other end of the leash.

The second half of the book will highlight the human elements and how to balance the relationship that you have with your dog.

We humans and our animals have all the elements in our person-alities. You may initially see several elements reflected in your dog. However, there will be one or two elements that clearly stand out. Once you identify your dog's predominant elements by observation of archetypal traits, finding their default emotions under stress, and numerous other clues, you can use your support tools of simple lifestyle measures to keep them balanced and happy. And it will also be easier to find your own element and create balance within your relationship.

Balance is always our main goal. We seek out the imbalance while striving to find and empower the balance.

The Five Element system is based on seasonal elemental change. Although you may have identified your dog's primary element you might see "seasonal" shades of the other elements during different times of the year. Dogs will show a whisper—or a shout—of the seasonal element that is currently in season. For example, Wood is a spring element. Many dogs will show some Wood-type traits during this season. As the season passes by they will however, always shift back to their predominant one or two elements. If needed you can use the support methods for each element in its "season"; however, your dog's predominant element support methods will be helpful to them all year round.

This is the seasonal cycle of the five elements: the cycle begins with the Wood element in spring, the Fire element in summer, the Earth element in late summer, the Metal element in autumn, and the Water element in winter.

Dog and human elements may also shift slightly with age. That is the normal cycle of life. Puppies are a moving elemental target and may or may not have a predominant element until they are about 12 months old. Senior dogs may add or drop an element as they age. Many dogs will have two strong elements. It is up to us to observe certain ingrained behaviors and traits, such as their reaction to stress, that show their predominant element. Completing all the quizzes in each element chapter will help you determine their element profile.

Water is the last seasonal cycle of the elements. The mysterious Water Dog shapeshifters show us all the elements as they see fit, at any given moment or whim, changing to a different element at the speed of light. That is how you know they are a Water element!

Many senior dogs will move into the Water element near the end of life. This quiet winter season is full of ancestral wisdom, powerful inner stillness, and an enduring soft strength—a nice way to be in elder years.

Here is a helpful glossary for some of the traditional Chinese medicine terms you will encounter in this book.

Table 1. Glossary of Chinese terms

Name	Symbol	Definition
Excess Joy	过剩的欢乐	A state of excessive excitement and agitation that can disturb and damage the Shen.
Heart Fire	心火	Excess heat in the Fire element that creates overstimulation.
Jing	景	The essence with which one comes into the world and slowly loses with age.
Qi (Chi)	齊	Life force energy.
Shen	沈	One's Spirit, the spiritual element of one's psyche, stored in the heart.
Disturbance of the Shen	申的擾亂	Anxiety, restlessness, panic, inability to focus.
Yin	英	The female energy in the universe: the dark, cold, wetness.
Yang	楊	The male energy in the universe: the light, warmth, dryness.
Yin and Yang	陰陽	A symbol of harmony and balance—two opposite but interconnected forces that dance together to create balance in all aspects of life.

Archetypes

*If you know your archetype— and not just yours, if you
know how to perceive the world in archetypes and through
archetypes—everything changes... Everything.*

— CAROLYN MYSS

Elements have archetypal energies that correlate to typical behaviors. We can refer to these as certain typical identities. For instance, the Wood element is the Army Sergeant, the Fire element is the Diva, the Earth element is the Nurturer, the Metal element is the Librarian, and finally, the Water element is the mystical Empath. Each archetype reflects distinct emotions, strengths, and weaknesses that are true to that element. Archetypes can also give us a quick reference tool when we are trying to gauge another being's element on the fly!

Below are generic definitions for the Five Element assessment tools. (Each dog element chapter goes into more detail.) This list gives you a definition of each aspect or trait we will be looking at to find our dog's predominant element. Think of them as clues to a furry puzzle!

Archetype: A typical identity that relates to each individual element.

Strengths: Superpowers, attributes, interesting and strange behaviors.

Emotional Default: Primary emotion created by stress and/or imbalance.

Season: Seasonal time frame of element for optimum strength and balance or weaknesses and imbalances.

Organs: Yin and yang organs energetically associated with each element.

Time: Each element's 24-hour time frame as affected by balance/imbalance. Time may relate to the functioning time of the element's corresponding physiological organ.

Sense Organ: Orifice/body opening that is used for sensing.

Sense: Sight, taste, smell, speech, or hearing; can be a superpower or impaired.

Coat Color: Typical coat colors are included; however, do not use this as your primary element assessment tool for dogs. Due to the many canine breeding variations, coat colors may or may not be accurate or typical in dogs. When coat is atypical for the suspected element, look to all the other indicators for primary element assessment.

Governed Part of Body: Body part most affected by the element.

Common Issues: Physical issues that may arise for each element.

Wants, Needs, Stressors, and Support

Properly trained, a man can be a dog's best friend.
— COREY FORD

We can further look for clues about our dog's element by dominant personality and behavior traits such as wants and needs, reactions to stress, and supportive measures, as shown in the list below.

Wants: Good to excellent options for maintaining balance in the element.

Needs: Necessary for maintaining balance and harmony.

Stressors: Things that create imbalance within each individual dog element.

Response to Stress: Emotional and physical response to stress.

Stress Balancers: Actions that bring relief and balance, often the same as wants and needs.

Supportive Therapies: Can be ways to help your dog that are related to physical action or emotional relationship.

Relationship Support: Pathways and actions that this element needs to feel safe and loved.

Life Lesson: Reflections of what each dog element can teach us.

On the following page you'll find a quick hybrid reference guide for all five dog elements.

Table 2. Quick reference guide for the five dog elements

Element	Archetype	Strength	Emotion	Season	Sense	Color	Issues	Needs	Stressors
WOOD	Competitor Army sergeant	Athletic Competitive	Anger	Spring	Sight	Black/ brown	Sinews Eyes	Movement	Lack of movement
FIRE	Party dog Diva	Social Friendly	Excess joy Shen	Summer	Speech	Red/white	Heart Heat Skin Stomach	Adoration Social	Chaos Alone Heat
EARTH	Caregiver	Kind Gentle Patient	Worry	Late summer	Taste	Yellow/tan Chubby	Digestive Weight Dental	Food! Routine Family	Off routine Alone
METAL	Librarian	Intelligent Sensitive Focused	Grief	Autumn	Smell	Grey Lean & Muscular	Skin Immune Respiratory	Work Quiet	Noise Losses
WATER	Empath	Sensitive Empathic Wise	Fear	Winter	Hearing	Black mix	Joints Kidney Bladder	Quiet Deep Connection	Chaos Envirotoxins Loud noises

NOTE: This is an abbreviated standard assessment framework for TCM's Five Element theory for dogs. This table is based on personality assessment with a few standard aspects that are important for discovering your dog's element. The extensive standard traditional framework (not shown here) gives TCM practitioners a roadmap to follow for acupuncture, acupressure, diet, and husbandry treatment protocols, which are not in the scope of this book.

Rescue Dogs and Shelter Applications:
More Than Just a Curiosity

As anyone who goes into dog rescue knows, it is not a
"for-profit" business, but the rewards are priceless.
— EMMYLOU HARRIS

Thankfully, many dog owners provide loving homes to rescue dogs. These dogs come from all walks of life and are often given up or rescued due to difficult circumstances. The one thing they all have in common is a prior lifetime of stress. Stress can actually be a helpful indicator of what each dog needs for a balanced life. When we can identify a dog's stressors, we can identify its element and learn more about the dog's personality, wants and needs, possible triggers, and desired lifestyle.

Shelter staff and kennel workers have keen senses and huge, strong hearts that often can detect a dog's stressors, their mechanisms for coping, and their general wants and needs. First responders out in the field picking up animals are the first ones to have a pulse on "who the dog is." This initial awareness can be the key to identifying how to handle and manage a frightened animal with, hopefully, a cooperative approach.

Approaching an animal and noticing how it reacts guides us in understanding its stress behavior reflex. Is it aggression, panic, worry, hiding, or deep visceral fear that turns into fear aggression? Each one of these comes from one of five unique archetypal reactions. All rescue personnel have a high sensitivity level for animals, ways of being and doing that work—until they don't.

Having the simple knowledge and wisdom of the dog's element can be a great help. How a dog reacts to stress is the first solid archetypal indicator; what each dog wants and needs follows from that. Understanding the dog's primary element can be valuable in calming the dog and working with it.

There are countless tools in this book for detecting a dog's element and strategies that soothe, calm, and balance dogs during the rescue process, in shelters, and in their move to their new home. Application of the Five Element theory is invaluable here.

The Five Element personality assessments can also be used to help these animals find the right humans and transition smoothly into their new home, hopefully their last home. With a few simple questions on an adopter's application, the perfect elemental human match can hopefully be made, and result in a lifetime of love and balanced care. As shelter staff work with the dog and get to know it, Five Element information can act as relationship counseling information and can be given to the new potential owner. To be able to categorize some of these aspects for rescue dogs will give them a better chance at finding and keeping the perfect forever home.

The Five Element theory is more than just a fun curiosity. It has the potential to change the lives of many animals in rescue situations, to find the right homes for them and help them stay in those homes. Sending home element profile information with a new, excited, big-hearted owner can ease the dog's transition, and create a solid understanding in that happy, forever home that we all desire for these animals.

I have personally utilized the Five Element techniques with the 17 rescue dogs that have been part of my life to date. They all became happy, well-adjusted, and balanced lifelong partners. We also integrate this into our humane wildlife and feral dog capture programs and teachings. It can be a powerful tool for creating harmony and saving lives.

Each dog element chapter has a section on Rescue dogs. I encourage everyone to read this, especially if you have adopted one. In Chapter 11 there is more information on the application of Five Element theory to rescue and shelter procedures. I truly hope we can all unite in sharing these tools for the well-being of animals around the world.

2. How to Use This Book

The detour I sent you was actually an upgrade.
You are welcome.

— THE UNIVERSE

This how-to chapter will give you a quick tour of the fundamentals for easily and successfully finding your dog's elements and your own human elements. Visit the following short sections before you dive into the dog element chapters. These short sections will provide the tools and basic directions for your fun Five Element search.

- First, be sure to bookmark **The Scenario**, starting on p. 29, and encode this short, active story in your mind's eye for a handy reference guide to each of the Five Element Dog Archetypes.

- Next, to find your primary elements, learn how to take and interpret the **Quizzes** for both your dog and you.

- **Father Time** is a quick overview of our Old Dog Element's requirements as they age. Their needs for support will gradually shift and this section shows how we can adapt for longevity and comfort.

- **Acupoints for Elemental Balance** gives you the parameters for doing easy, safe, and effective acupressure specific to your dog's element. Please bookmark the pages to reference during your acupressure sessions. Each dog element chapter will have two points to use for balancing your dog. There is also a Bonus! technique at the end of this chapter, so be sure to try that out too!

- **Chapter 8: Now, Who Are You?** will guide you through finding your own primary and additional elements and has tips for creating relationship balance with your element combination and your dog's element combination.

☸ **Chapter 9: The Weaving of Relationships** and **Chapter 10: Balancing and Blending for Harmony** will answer many relationship questions and give you tools to eliminate issues that may arise. All this will give you a solid foundation to zoom through life sleuthing out Who's Who, while creating balance and harmony, and supporting relationships with compassion, empathy, and respect. This is practical, effective, and fun advice that I've seen change lives time and time again.

☸ **Chapter 11: Rescue and Shelter** has tips that will help shelter workers and rescue organizations.

☸ Finally, **Chapter 12: The Happy Wagging Tail** is a Love Letter to Dogs. This short chapter holds our vision and flight path for the wings of our Five Element expansion.

☸ **The Resources** at the end of the book will support you in even more wisdom and knowledge from others. Be sure to check these out.

A final note… It takes a village… The suggestions in this book will be greatly enhanced if you have a supportive team of a Five Element acupuncturist or acupressure professional, a progressive dog trainer, a qualified animal bodyworker, an animal communicator, your own clear observation skills, persistence and patience, and as always, a knowledgeable, kind, and open-minded veterinarian for your support when needed.

The Scenario

Everyone thinks they have the best dog.
And none of them are wrong.
—W.R. PURSCHE

Five people lead their dogs into an obedience class…
- The first dog, brawny, brown, and black, struts in, pulling a bit on the leash while assessing the "competition" around him with a confident air.
- In bursts the second dog like a flash of fiery red, who pulls at the end of his leash and excitedly wags his whole body, eagerly turning to say hello to everyone and anyone.

- The third dog, a bit pudgy and yellow, looks to his handler with worried eyes and nuzzles the handler's treat bag, while happily wagging his tail and trying to ignore the flashy red dog.
- The fourth dog is lean, angular, greyish tan, and walks quietly along the handler's side paying absolute perfect attention to the bubble of his owner and himself.
- And lastly the fifth dog, mostly black with a long back, comes in slowly and quietly, head down, eyes up, walking slightly behind the handler, aware of every movement around her and yet confident—until she is not.

Each of these five scenario dogs represents the common behavioral characteristics associated with the five elements of traditional Chinese medicine. This mini preview spotlights the overall differences between the dog elements.

NOTE: In this scenario there were typical coat colors for each element. However, because there is so much variety in dog breeding for coat colors and combinations, this may or may not be relevant. Do not use coat color as your primary clue to the dog's element. Look more towards personality, behavior under stress, and needs and wants of your dog to determine his/her element. Be sure to visually encode the scenario in your mind for quick future reference!

Quizzes

Do you have any idea how much an elephant drinks?

—SARA GRUEN, author of Water for Elephants

Included in each individual Dog Element chapter is a short quiz. I recommend that you take ALL the quizzes.

Each element chapter has a quiz to find the primary element for both your dog and you. Just like every leaf on a tree is slightly different, every dog and human is made up of a diverse combination of elements. The quiz results will guide you to your dog's primary element and yours. This will help create understanding, acceptance, and tolerance for both your motivations and actions in your relationship, while giving you some tools for managing stress reactions and needs in your everyday life together. To be successful with the quiz it is important to rate the overall "consistent archetypal personality" for each element. There may be times when your dog is affected by a seasonal element or a certain circumstance where they may take on an element "mask" to use as a coping mechanism. They usually change back to their primary element once the season or circumstance has passed. The same is true for you.

Once you find your dog's and your primary element, go back and reread that element chapter. This will reinforce your understanding of the primary challenges you may face and the possible solutions for creating more harmony between your dog and yourself.

It is important to complete all the element quizzes so you can truly see the unique combination of elements for your dog. The secondary and third elements will also show themselves in the numbers, guiding you to your dog's and your own individual personality.

> **NOTE:** Remember that Water elements will seem complicated to assess but actually are easy once you recognize the main clue: Water can effectively mask all elements at any given time. Every day they can be a different element. That's how you know you have a Water element!

When completing each quiz, rate each question from 1 to 3:

1. Never true
2. Sometimes true
3. Always true

When you have finished, add up the scores and compare them with the other Five Element scores to see your dog's and your element profiles.

> And be sure to check out the Resource Section to find out how much an elephant drinks!

Father Time

*I can't think of anything that brings me closer to tears
than when my Old Dog—completely exhausted after a hard
day in the field—limps away from her nice spot in front
of the fire and comes over to where I'm sitting and puts her
head in my lap, a paw over my knee, and closes her eyes,
and goes back to sleep. I don't know what I've done to deserve
that kind of friend.*

—GENE HILL

Our Old Dogs never really lose their deeply embedded primary element traits. These traits may soften due to Father Time's influence and changes in mobility, or may seem to shift to a different element with the seasons. If we begin the element journey with the Wood element in springtime when new life is beginning and bursting forth, we can follow the elemental cycle through both the five yearly seasons and the seasons of life.

In the winter season of an animal or human's life, they may take on the final element in the elemental cycle, which is Water. We will still see sprinkles of their primary elements in their personality and behavior; however, the Water element stage will often be their final element. Water is the source and sustenance of all life and carries our Jing or life force energy.

A younger primary Water element animal can be a raging river, powerfully wearing down and smoothing stones in its path. An elder Water may manifest as a quiet, peaceful, reflective pool. Our Jing or life essence promotes growth, development, and reproduction, and it diminishes with age. We can often see this in grey muzzles and greying hair. Elder dogs will also exhibit stagnant Qi or life force energy. We notice this when they need more sleep, less movement, and overall less flow with life.

Water elements can easily walk between the worlds. These wise, soul-deep Water elders just may be "testing the waters" for their final transition.

Our Old Dogs will have their own unique elemental challenges and individual support methods. Their aspects of wants, needs, and stressors are more geriatric in nature. The use of supportive elemental balancers will help soften the process of aging and social withdrawal. Father Time will always have his way with our Old Dogs, but keen awareness and elemental support can promote a harmonious aging process.

Consistent consideration of our Old Dog's changing needs can help them feel balanced, happy, connected, and loved. The Five Element system has so much to offer our beloved Old Dogs!

Some Final Notes on All Old Dog Elements

Change is a difficult thing for our Old Dogs, particularly a household change. It can precipitate a downward spiral in their aging as weak senses, such as sight and smell have to readapt to a new "normal," creating stress on the body, mind, and spirit. I have watched this happen many times in my practice. If you don't have to move, don't. If you do have to move, try to mitigate by keeping dog beds, food bowls, and furniture in similar rooms, next to similar furniture or appliances while keeping their smells the same.

This can help them better navigate in their new home. Also keep their rhythms the same for feeding and walkies. The more you can keep the same—or design to feel the same—the better your Old Dog will adapt. Be sure to give them plenty of extra attention during these changes to lower their stress. They will need that support more than you know.

NOTE: Also, by utilizing P.A.C.K. (Patience, Acceptance, Compassion, and Kindness) along with the tenets of the Five Element balancers, we can greatly enrich our senior dogs' lives as well as our own. Remember that P.A.C.K. allows patience, acceptance, compassion, and kindness to be used with a single word and a single breath. It beautifully dovetails with the Five Element tools. Hold P.A.C.K. in your heart and use it regularly with your Old Dogs! (See Elizabeth's TEDx talk – "4 Life Lessons from our Old Dogs".)

General Information for Old Dog Elements

Stressors: Aging and environmental changes that prevent or inhibit elemental balance—individual to each dog element.

Response to Stress: Emotional/activity responses to stress.

Stress Balancers: Actions that bring relief and balance, often the same as wants and needs.

Relationship Support: Pathways and actions we can do that make our Old Dog element feel safe, important, and loved.

Life Lesson: Take home message of what we can learn from each individual Old Dog element.

Acupoints for Elemental Balance

At the tail-end of each dog element chapter you will have two helpful acupoints that are overall balancers for that element, with photos to help navigate the body and find the points. Please read through the important information below so you can safely and easily find the points and make the process an enjoyable and effective time for both you and your dog.

There is also a bonus technique for your dog at the end of this chapter—the Good Morning Spinal Wake-Up. Check it out. Your dogs will love it!

How Does Acupressure Work?

- It's all about Qi = Life Force Energy. We all have it!
- Qi can be balanced or imbalanced, and affects many aspects of the body, mind, and spirit.
- Balanced Qi = health, vitality, and harmony; imbalanced Qi = dullness, emotionality, fatigue, illness.
- There are 12 meridians with over 360 acupressure points on the body.
- Acupoints are areas of activity along the meridians where Qi flows, like bus stops for integrating energy and healing.
- Each point can promote a different action in the body.

- Your touch creates an energy exchange with the animal's Qi. There is a piezoelectric charge that happens and electrical responses move through the cells and tissues of the body (this is measurable by science).

- Some points relax, some points stimulate, some points support organs and digestion, aid in pain control, and so much more.

- Ancient "How" – Use it Now!

Healing Rooted in the Spirit

凡大醫治病，必當安神定志，無欲無求，
先發大慈惻隱之心。誓願普救含靈之苦。

Whenever eminent healers treat an illness, they must quiet the spirit and settle the will, they must be free of wants and desires, and they must first develop a heart full of great compassion and empathy. They must pledge to devote themselves completely to relieving the suffering of all sentient beings.

— Sun Simiao, Bei Ji Qian Jin Yao Fang 1.2
(as translated by Sabine Wilms)

Figure 1: Healing Rooted in the Spirit

Tips for Successful Acupressure Sessions

First prepare yourself:

- Check in with your own inner state: Are you quiet and calm? Or stressed? Sad? Angry?
- Take three deep breaths.
- Find calmness and rest in it.
- Be grounded and present.
- Open your heart and smile—you just balanced your Qi!

Then prepare your dog:

- Check in with your animal. Are they quiet and calm? Relaxed? Receptive? High energy? Or stressed?
- Work in a calm and relaxing area, or a favorite cuddle spot.
- Limit any distractions for the animal and you if possible.
- Best not to do acupressure close to or before normal feeding or playtime.

- Practicing at a time when the animal is calmer will bring more success.

Finding the Acupressure Points

- Have your source materials available.
- You do not need to be perfectly accurate – if unsure widen your scope of touch to the general area, the animal's body will respond.
- In traditional Chinese medicine it is poetically said that the points are most often found in the valleys, not on the mountains.
- Be sure to BREATHE, the animal will be on alert if you are holding your breath.
- Your breath also moves Your Qi!

DISCLAIMER: Acupressure is not meant to replace veterinary care, is not meant for diagnosis or to treat disease. Be sure to consult your veterinarian if you suspect a health problem, or prior to the use of acupressure if your animal has a serious health problem. Acupressure is meant to complement veterinary medicine with your veterinarian's permission. Initially working with a skilled veterinary acupressure and/ or acupuncture practitioner is recommended.

Do not use these points on pregnant animals!
If you suspect your animal is pregnant refrain from acupressure unless you are working with a qualified veterinary acupuncturist or are trained above the introductory level of acupressure by an experienced instructor.

Point Technique, Pressure, and Response

- Locate the point on your source material.
- Gently stroke the area with a flat hand two or three times.
- Feel for the "divot" or acupoint; most points are in hollows.
- Place two fingers on the point with gentle, soft pressure.
- Breathe! Don't think too much, be relaxed.
- Sink in slowly and softly and hold the point for 30–60 seconds or rub gently.

- Watch/listen to your animal's responses and adjust pressure as needed.
- Too little may tickle, too deep may be tender.
- Your animal may yawn, lick, sneeze, or stretch; this is normal and suggests a release of endorphins in the body.
- When you feel you are done, gently stroke the region again to "seal" the energy in.
- Respecting your animal's tolerance is a dynamic part of deeply "connecting" with your animal.

What's Next?

Options are:

- Repeat the same point on the other side of the body.
- Do a different point.
- Finish for the day. If you are short on time or the animal has had enough or you just feel done, stop there! Always end things on a good note.
- You may need to ease into this work with some animals, as they may not be able to decompress enough at first to take it all in. Be patient, only do one point or technique. Even one point will help!

Do not use acupressure if:

- Your animal is ill or injured and you haven't consulted the veterinarian.
- The animal has a fever.
- The area is around a sensitive or open wound.
- The area has acute heat or swelling.
- Your animal is pregnant and you have not consulted the veterinarian.
- There is a contagious condition.
- There are cancerous tumors, unless consulting the veterinarian.
- Your animal has eaten a large meal; wait one half hour before you begin.

BONUS!!

I like to do the Good Morning Spinal Wake-Up first thing in the morning or before the other techniques in each dog element chapter. This is great for dogs of all ages, but especially the geriatrics and dogs in recovery.

> NOTE! Be gentle with your pressure as these points can be tender at first.

This technique literally wakes up three important systems:

- It stimulates the neuro-lymphatic points along the spine and gets the lymph fluid moving after a night's rest.
- It also wakes up the "Shu" acupressure points along the spine that connect with every acupuncture meridian and the nerves to every organ in the body. These Shu points are like circuit breaker switches that turn everything on.
- Lastly, it brings blood flow into the muscles that surround the spinal column, which helps with flexibility and pain. This is great for dogs of all ages, but especially for geriatric dogs and dogs in recovery.

This technique starts a gentle but significant cascade of circulation amongst these three systems and only takes 30 to 45 seconds.

Figure 2: Good Morning Spinal Wake-Up

This technique is best done first thing in the morning, with the dog standing or sitting. My dogs line up for it every morning!

1. Begin just behind the shoulder blades. Hold your thumb and forefinger one to two inches apart and position each finger along opposite sides of the spine. The size of your dog will determine the width of your fingers.

2. Sink in with gentle pressure and while in place, wiggle your fingers front to back. Think wiggle, wiggle, wiggle.

3. Next, slide back approximately one-half to one inch (less for small dogs) and you will naturally fall into a little divot along the sides of the vertebrae.

4. Wiggle, wiggle, wiggle in place a few times again and slide back.

5. Repeat until you reach the pelvis area where you will not feel any more vertebrae.

6. Repeat the whole process three times. Watch your dog limber up and smile!

The rest of the acupressure points are located at the end of each dog element chapter. You can use them one to three times per week or as needed for balance and harmony.

Use them with joy!

PLEASE REMEMBER! Do not use these points on pregnant animals!

This is just the beginning of a vast amount of information about each dog element that you will find in the chapters ahead. Each of the following five chapters on the individual dog elements includes in-depth information and real-life stories with human element and relationship chapters to follow.

Now, let's find out who's who!

PART 2
The Element Dog

3. The Wood Dog

*What is rooted is easy to nourish, what is brittle is easy
to break, what is recent is easy to correct, what is small
is easy to scatter.*
—TAO TE JING (CHAPTER 72).

*"The first dog, brawny, brown and black, struts in,
pulling a bit on the leash..."*

Characteristics of a Wood Dog

Movement is a Wood Dog's medicine. These dogs thrive on competition and are athletic and powerful. In the human world we often relate the Wood element archetype to being an army sergeant or a world class competitor. They are courageous, alert, and very aware. Their senses, especially sight, are always turned on and highly tuned to react if needed. Many athletes, working police dogs, or military dogs are Wood elements. A famous Wood element dog was "Rin Tin Tin." They are unflinching under pressure, push beyond limits and fear, and will take charge if they see a weakness or an opening.

Wood Dogs are very grounded, like the trees they reflect in the nature-based Five Element theory. They become deeply rooted in their purposes and goals, are alive with determination, and offer the fruits of benevolence to those that listen. Wood Dogs are solid under pressure and yet flexible with the winds of change. This makes them excellent working dogs and athletes. Wood Dogs are truly devoted to their caregiver or working partner and develop deep bonds that endure through the many storms of life.

Like most trees, Wood elements need seasonal rest time and will develop a deeply rooted maturity during that time, usually winter.

Wood Element Dogs

Personality characteristics and support for well-being and balance

Archetype	Army sergeant or upper-level competitor
Strengths	Athletic, competitive, leader, fast learner, benevolent
Emotional default	Anger, frustration, aggression, impatience
Season	Spring
Organs	Gallbladder, liver
Time	11:00 p.m. – 1:00 a.m. and 1:00 a.m. – 3:00 a.m.
Sense organ	Eyes
Sense	Sight
Coat color	Often brown and black
Common issues	Tendon and ligament issues, eye issues, muscle tension
Wants	Movement, variety, competition
Needs	Clear boundaries from human partner, movement, variety, challenge, gentle kindness and appreciation
Stressors	Inconsistent rules and boundaries, boredom
Response to stress	Frustration, impatience, anger
Stress balancers	Consistent boundaries, clear leadership, challenging and varied work, gentle kindness and soft praise
Supportive therapies	Massage, acupressure, swimming, movement, adjunct herbal support
Relationship support	Stay present, clear-headed, and fully engaged when working with Wood Dogs. Maintain solid boundaries and competent, kind leadership. *Do not use force; it will backfire on you!*

As they rest through winter, the seasonal effects of the Water element provide Wood with deep nurturing and potentiates energy and growth. In the season of spring, the Wood element season, the Wood Dog will burst forth with power and drive, ready for all challenges. Watch for their readiness, vigilance, and strength when the spring seedlings start sprouting!

The Story of Ivar

I've worked on numerous Wood element police and military dogs. One police dog close to retirement, a very handsome black Polish shepherd named Ivar, stands out for me. He was always working, even while I was working on him. In his monthly bodywork tune-ups, he would hand himself over by relaxing his muscles and participating with my requested movements, but his senses, mainly eyes and nose, were constantly working and scanning his surroundings. He was in a relaxed state of permanent hypervigilance! Animals, when having bodywork, often show tissue and energetic release by yawning, stretching, or licking their lips. I had to pay constant attention to Ivar's signals. Every so often I would catch a barely noticeable smacking of the lips to suggest that we were making headway or that something felt good. I was grateful to his handler for offering feedback that our work had in fact helped his gait shift back to normal and lessened his chronic pain.

I curiously asked Ivar's human partner if Ivar ever slept. He said he didn't know as every time he woke up, Ivar was staring at him. I treated Ivar for about a year and it was mostly business for him. Eventually I began getting a hello from him consisting of two tail wags with a quick glance before he would assume the position for his bodywork session and become Ivar the police dog again. I felt extremely honored for those two wags and that quick glance. I also asked his handler if Ivar played much. His handler laughed and said he demanded his play session after each work day, no matter how hard or long the day was. So, there was some balance there! Ivar was a working dog that truly embodied and loved his job, his partnership, and having fun!

The Wood Dog usually ranks high in the "pack" in most circumstances where there are multiple dogs, such as dog parks and competitions. They will also dominate at home if they do not have a strong human or animal leader. Wood Dogs (and Wood people) will often step into a leadership role if there is no solid leader evident. It's common for Wood Dogs to test us humans regularly, just to be sure someone is in charge. I have, however, seen Wood Dogs bow down to Earth, Metal, and Fire element cats! In the Five Element Sheng (creation) and Ko (control) cycles, Earth and Water support Wood's roots and growth, Metal cuts Wood, and Fire burns Wood. Those dynamics can create a healthy respect in the Wood Dog no matter how small the other animal elements are!

Wood Dogs are independent and determined yet also need clear boundaries from their human handlers. Boundaries are not bad things for Wood Dogs. Being of a naturally competitive nature, boundaries give the Wood Dog something to push against for growth. Steady boundaries will also harness their energy for success. As any athlete knows, what makes us get really good at something is the actual readiness and striving for the next challenge. A human partner who is aware, clear, and consistent, utilizing firm boundaries, will easily earn respect from a Wood Dog. The handler must also respect, recognize, and time the expansion of the Wood Dog's boundaries so he can continue to become the very best version of himself.

Many moons ago, a very talented and well-known dog trainer told me that "smart" dogs learn bad behaviors as quickly as they learn good behaviors, so I should be very clear and focused when working with them. I had acquired my first, very smart Wood Dog. I had done healing work on many very smart and talented Wood Dogs, but I had not had one for a life partner. I am predominantly a Water element with some Wood and Fire thrown in. When all my elements are balanced (HA HA!) my Water can feed a Wood element and make them grow, my Wood can create a mutual Wood to Wood understanding, and my Fire aspect can be fed by wood when needed, creating focus and determination.

The Story of Max

Max, my Wood Dog, was my benevolent mentor. In all his wisdom, Max helped me learn how to grow within our Five Element relationship. The Wood element is related to the season of spring, a time of fresh burgeoning growth pushing the limits to become whatever it is meant to be. It is a time of grounded, powerful energy. Watching Max's Wood element shape itself taught me how to manage and balance my boundary-less, empathic Water while channeling and growing my own Wood element. Max taught me how to live in the present moment while being solidly connected to him and the earth below me. Thanks to Max, I learned a valuable lesson about the importance of grounding myself.

He also taught me to step up and recognize my own buried potential for my Wood element by demanding "real-time" confidence in any situation—both in him and in me. Waters don't always operate in "real-time." Each time my Water would flow and expand into an overly powerful, spread-out flood tide, his Wood medicine dammed me back up and calmed me to a quiet, present, focused pool. When my regular flood tides occurred, he clearly showed me my Water imbalance by being overly protective of me—my signal for seeing my own personal stress or fear—and by demanding more movement, training, or challenges. Basically, refocusing and re-rooting me to "our" world right now, right under my feet. Max would take charge in a benevolently cooperative way when I couldn't.

My rebalanced Water element energy would then be free to feed both his and my own amazing Wood energy with Water's inner stillness, endurance, connection, powerful yet soft strength, and deep wisdom. My Water's ability for potent focus and devotional flow held a vessel for his growth, fed his determination, and bolstered his confidence and willingness to learn and excel. It also helped me learn to navigate my own competitive Wood element. At the time, I was competing in water sports, racing sailboats and outrigger canoes. I was a strong competitor, and a helmswoman. I was also a business owner as well as doing search and rescue work. Max and I both learned and grew together, creating an elemental balance and deep awareness of both our partnership and who we each were. The timing was perfect for both of us to become the best versions of ourselves.

Funny thing, I ended up marrying a Wood/Water element and we dance the same dance that Max taught me way back when. Only now, the only competition is who has to do the dishes!

Best Practices for Working with Wood Dogs

Wood Dogs require us as handlers and partners to have strong focus, confidence, solid leadership, and real-time connection, creating a real working partnership. Yes, we can play and cuddle and have Wood Dog parties but only on our "off" time. Strong Wood element people do great with Wood Dogs. They understand and vibrate on the same levels of determination and competition when both dog and human are balanced. It may not be pretty though when either or both Wood elements become imbalanced.

Wood Dogs are very fast, eager learners and typically, like a tree, very grounded and invested in their growth and learning. When training, they may become impatient or irritable if there is an ungrounded or distracted handler, too much repetition, or if the Wood Dog is imbalanced in other areas of life, usually caused from lack of enough movement and challenge. Honoring their need to move will make any training easier, so first give them a good run, play, or a long walk. They will be more focused and less impatient with the more methodical acts of training. Smart animals don't appreciate too much repetition!

Do not over-train either; brief reviews of known basics are all these Wood Dogs typically need. They will feel good about themselves as they rapidly fire responses back to you and then ask, "Can we move on now?" Keep the challenges flowing for them but hold the boundaries until they are truly ready for that next challenge. They want to succeed. They also really do not respect the "woohoo party" praise while working. Quiet praise that comes directly from your heart and pride in them is all they need; then move on. The woohoo party will be welcome when they are done working.

Movement, competition, and challenge are the Wood Dog's main goals and there are many ways to fill that need. Agility has all the components they love: challenge, speed, movement, variety, and competition. Nose work, backpacking, skijoring, and doggie water sports are also good possibilities. Search and rescue, policework, conservation scent detection work, and security work are all viable avenues to fill their needs. However, these may not be suited for the average home life. If you suspect that you have a strong Wood element dog that is always trying to protect you or challenge you, try harnessing that energy into a different direction by giving them more movement, more challenges, and even sports if possible. Give them a job—they need and love that.

If your Wood Dog is working or competing he will most certainly be pushing himself to the absolute limits of his body, so be sure you are supporting his performance with healthy food, massage, chiropractic, acupressure, and supplements, particularly after competitions or good, hard fun.

Wood Dogs respond extremely well to herbal remedies. Spring season is a time of high potency for most herbs as well as a high potency time for our Wood Dogs. The seasonal synergy and power of herbs and Wood Dogs, both at their fullest strength, allows for a kindred energetic match that has a potent influence on healing and support. Be sure to work with a qualified animal herbalist or veterinarian when choosing remedies.

A while back, I did some testing for Working Dogs for Conservation, in Bozeman, Montana. The organization only accepts high-energy rescue dogs that have been rehomed too many times and do not have many or any options left ahead of them. The dogs are tested for their aptitude for scent work, focus, energy levels, and drive. I placed two rescue dogs with WDC. Both excelled during testing for intelligence, rapid learning style, drive, determination, and high energy levels. They were both strong Wood elements.

The Stories of Timber and Wally

One was a determined, high-energy, blind from birth, Labrador retriever named Timber. Sight is the sense organ for the Wood element and although Timber acted like a pure Wood element, he was missing his primary elemental sense organ. Timber's determination, drive, and working dog nature were off the charts—classic Wood! He never stopped hunting, and was absolutely amazing at scent work, so good that I triple tested and videoed him before offering him to WDC. Each test score was absolutely perfect and Timber never tired of the work. Accepting him was a big step for WDC as they had never adopted a blind scent dog before. It made sense, however, that his already powerful canine nose would be even more enhanced by his lack of sight.

Timber came to me as a blind, misunderstood Wood Dog with energy to spare. After proving his talent, he was flown to Canada to become a very successful invasive mussel sniffing dog. He spent his days with his loving and talented handler, sniffing for invasive mussels on the bottoms of boats prior to entering lakes around the region. Timber was fulfilling his purpose despite his so-called "handicap and wild nature." I'm sure he had a lot of fun Labrador swim time too!

The second dog I chose was a stocky, solid little mixed breed with extremely high energy and drive to spare, who also excelled at his testing. Wally loved to crawl into tight spots for searches just because he could. He got excited about anything and everything you gave him to channel his awesome Wood energy into. He was definitely not a dog for normal home life due to his near explosive energy. Wally had been returned to shelters and rehomed numerous times and WDC was his last chance. Like all Wood elements, his determination was huge and all that energy needed to be channeled. Wally was especially good at detailed vehicle searches and would indicate the exact location of the hidden target, never moving off the target until his handler allowed it. Thankfully, he is still working in Zambia with several other WDC dogs, sniffing for ivory poachers at police vehicle stops and has near 100% success with his target finds. The WDC dogs have a securely protected compound with cozy housing and even a very large doggie swimming pool for cooling off. Another misunderstood Wood with a mission in life to better the world!

Common Ailments in Wood Dogs

The common ailments and body parts affected by imbalances in the Wood Dog are tendon and ligament injuries, muscle soreness, liver issues, digestive problems, and eye conditions. The liver, a Wood element's yin organ, resides on the right side of the body. For Wood elements it is common that the right side of the body is more affected with muscle tension and stiffness. Movement can both help and hinder most of these issues. Consult your veterinarian on all the above. Keeping a regular exercise program with warm-up and cool-downs for your Wood Dog will keep his muscles strong, meaning fewer tendon or ligament tears and less stiffness.

The most important health need, mentally and physically, for the Wood Dog or any Wood Dog combination is movement. Give them plenty of walks or runs. Don't skimp on their time playing, working, or training or you will have an overactive and impatient Wood Dog on your hands. They are athletically gifted animals and need that movement and challenge to create elemental balance and harmony.

The Wood Dog's need for movement plays an important role in their overall health. The Wood element's yin organ, the liver, has the task of cleaning house in the body. Active movement helps the liver flush toxins better while balancing the Wood element Qi. Movement activates and accelerates the pumping of blood to all the sinews and muscles while cleansing the entire body. The liver Qi will become congested without this daily active movement and imbalances will follow. This can lead to aggression, impatience, property destruction, and a lack of trust and connection between the handler and animal. Keep them exercised and challenged in both body and mind to avoid this.

If your dog is waking you up between 1:00 a.m. and 3:00 a.m. each night, there is a good chance that the Wood/Liver Qi is imbalanced. As movement pumps the blood through the liver during the day, toxins can accumulate in the liver; the liver then completes its nightly job of cleansing and approximately 500 other bodily processes. The 24-hour clock time for the liver to perform its toxin cleansing and other magic is when we are typically asleep, between 1:00 and 3:00 a.m.

In Chinese medicine, a congested or imbalanced liver can be associated with stored and often inappropriate anger. This can cause aggression, impatience, and frustration. Anger is a Wood Dog's archetypal stress response and can be balanced by giving them regular active movement along with Wood element-appropriate lifestyle measures. Consistent boundaries, competent leadership, challenging work and exercise, variation in life experiences and of course, fun, praise, and kindness will create needed balance within the Wood Dog.

Balancing the Wood Dog's Qi in this way while utilizing supportive therapies for their incredible athleticism can keep your Wood Dog happy and healthy, with clear focused energy to spare and a strong drive to be the best they can be.

Wood Dog Life Lesson
Stay clear-headed and fully connected with your Wood Dog to avoid power struggles.

Wood Element Rescue Dogs – Misunderstood Stars

Wood rescue dogs are often rehomed numerous times due to their natural high energy and absolute need for physical activity, challenge, and mental stimulus. These animals have an instinctive drive to move, compete, protect, alert, learn, and work. They are determined beings and highly intelligent. When these natural drives are not fulfilled, the byproducts of Wood's innate emotional reflex of anger may come out. This can show as frustration, irritability, impatience, and aggression, all due to insufficient exercise, lack of stimulus, and lack of challenge. Wood Dogs tend strongly towards being high-energy dogs and need an outlet or some way to focus that energy in a solid, safe direction. Sadly, it may not always be the best direction.

Wood Dogs will typically create a job or an outlet if they don't have one. That may be as clear and simple as fiercely protecting children or adults in the household or as abstract as jumping fences, barking regularly, property destruction, and non-responsiveness to known prior training. This often shows a lack of handler leadership, which this dog needs and craves. Without clear, consistent leadership they will become the leader. This is an imbalance in both the relationship and each individual—both dog and handler.

Wood Dogs are best rescued by people with active lifestyles, or who are engaged in working dog programs such as search and rescue, police work, scent detection work, or competitive canine sports such as agility, scent work, and water sports. They will get along well with Wood element humans that have an athletic lifestyle that includes consistent daily exercise such as running, hiking, backpacking, regular travel, swimming—anything that moves the Wood Dog's amazing body and stimulates their incredible mind.

If you have adopted a Wood Dog, introducing them to their new home may take some patience at first. Often, rescues come to new owners with an unknown or very little history. Spend the time to learn what they want and like to do. Work with a qualified trainer with the goal of becoming a solid partner and competent leader for this animal. Yes, you can be both! Be clear, present, fair, and available to them. Find and give them the boundaries they seek. Find a job or challenge for them to focus on and sustain your partnership when working with them. Take them with you as often as possible. Sight is the natural sense for a Wood Dog. Allow them to exercise this sense too.

Their needs are actually fairly simple in the right home and they will become eternally devoted partners with the right awareness, leadership, and handling. Wood Dogs are worth the effort and have a lot to teach us about ourselves and our lifestyles.

Wood Dog Quiz	
1 = Never true | 2 = Sometimes true | 3 = Always true	
	I am happiest when I get movement each day
	I get impatient when I am learning the same thing over and over
	I often have muscle tightness
	I love to compete
	I am happiest with a structured daily program
	I am not afraid of conflict with other animals or humans
	I have an extremely strong will to succeed
	I am always courageous and never show fear
	I like to know exactly where all my toys, gear, and handler are
	I am highly determined to succeed
	I am hardworking
	I love challenges
	I am incredibly devoted and loyal to my handler
	I will fiercely protect my humans and friends
	I perform very well under stress
	I am confident
	I am a good communicator of my needs or problems
	I notice and don't like bad people
	I can find it difficult to relax or "turn off"
	I want and need a job and am best as a working dog with one partner
	Wood Element Dog Total

The Old Wood Dog

The Wood Dog does not take getting old gracefully. He is not used to limitations with his body and will often be incredibly frustrated and grumpy as aging limits his physical abilities. His mind is still raring to go and along with his strong determination and drive, can wreak havoc on his aging body.

The Old Wood Dog will be happiest if you create challenges for him. Nose work is a great option as it's a low-level exercise with limited movement, and challenging, self-competitive, and fun! Almost any Old Dog can do nose work and feel a sense of accomplishment and renewal. It relieves boredom and gives them something to look forward to. It gives the Old Wood element dogs that sense of being of value along with the challenge they still need. Georgia Edwards M.D., a retired oncologist turned canine nose work instructor, says: "Nose work is the one fun game that all dogs can do until the end of their life." Once you learn the basics from a qualified nose work trainer you can easily do this at home. You may even feed the Wood Dog's competitive nature by entering nose work competitions. Your Old Wood Dog will be begging for the opportunity to "search" or "find it."

Our Old Wood Dogs need outlets for their innate drive and energy, even if their body is complaining and not performing like it used to. Providing these outlets comes with the responsibility of having a Wood Dog in your life. It can be fun and rewarding for both of you.

I had the pleasure recently to work with a strong Old Wood element dog, a noble Portuguese Water Dog (PWD) named Spirit Bojangles. Bo had the natural drive of a competitor. You could feel it in his body and spirit, and see it in his eyes. Bo was classified a Veteran CPE Agility Trial Champion when I met him at a PWD water trials competition. As I worked on him he would gaze out at all the other competitors as if to see how they measured up. You could feel the excited tension in his body to get back in the water and show off. It is always an honor to work on these veteran athletes; it touches my heart with pride.

In his final days on the planet, Bo achieved an elite Agility title, his CS-ATE Specialist title, which meant he was a Specialist Agility Team Extraordinaire! Bo's strong Wood determination and lifelong athleticism allowed him to still do the tunnels, weaves, jumps, and a very tough obstacle run to achieve his title, with points to spare. He aced it! Bo and his little competitor buddy, a cavalier spaniel named "Messy," both earned big, tough titles that day. The two champions and their proud moms celebrated with a yummy meatball party afterward. Bo is now a hero among the famous and elite agility dogs and left his mom with a warm smile in her heart. Wood Dogs often have careers to be remembered by.

Movement is still an Old Wood Dog's medicine—in moderation. As they continue to age, multiple short walks with a variety of scenery and smells will be an effective way to counter stiffness and keep their mind and nose stimulated, their sight/brain connection strong, and their emotions in check.

Just like in humans, regular varied stimulus can help slow down cognitive decline for our aging dogs. Wood elements are highly susceptible to sight stimulus as this is their elemental sense organ. As they age, they continue to benefit from the sight stimulation of regular walks, especially in various locations. Multiple short walks in both familiar and unfamiliar forests or venues will support their need for sight and scent stimulation. New areas and new venues of sight stimulus continue to create new connections in the brain. I believe that all our Old element dogs can benefit from regular varied sight, scent, and auditory stimulus and live a happier, healthier life with us as they age.

Teaching your fast learner Old Wood Dog some easy new tricks will keep him engaged and feeling successful. There are several great books about this. Enrichment activities are abundant. Finding what "gently challenges" your aging Wood Dog may be a simplified version of an event or play style that he loved and found success with in his early life. He will always need to be successful at something to be happy and balanced.

As with most Old Dogs, continued senior support of acupressure and massage will help tremendously with stiffness and pain. Targeted herbal remedies can also be helpful and of course buckets of praise and love!

Life Lesson from the Old Wood Dog
Gently treat him like the warrior that his heart still is, with respect, partnership, and plenty of genuine, awestruck praise.

Issues for Older Wood Dogs

Old Dog Stressors: Boredom, lack of movement, physical limitations.

Response to Stress: Grumpiness, frustration, stiffness, apathy.

Stress Balancers: Mental stimulation, frequent walks and exercise while tapering duration and increasing frequency, walks in both familiar and new locations, games, nose work, farm dog competitions, massage, acupressure, herbal remedies, gentle play.

Relationship Support: Be patient, kind and consistent, take them everywhere with you for sight/brain stimulation needs. Make them feel successful at small things!

Acupressure Points
for the Wood Dog

Please take a moment to refer to the guidelines for acupressure in Chapter 2, page 34.

CAUTION: Do not use these points on pregnant animals!

Gall Bladder 21 (GB 21) "Shoulder Well" relaxes and releases the muscles, tendons, and ligaments in the body. This point is wonderful for hard-working Wood Dogs. It also helps balance the gastrointestinal tract, ease emotions such as anger, frustration, and impatience, and calms the mind. This point is located just in front of the dog's scapula (shoulder blade) and from top to bottom in the middle of the muscle in front of it; see top image on the next page (Figure 3).

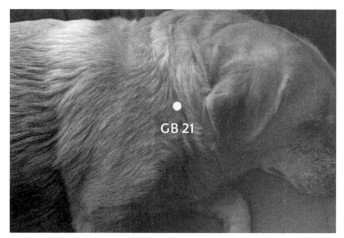

Figure 3: Gall Bladder (GB 21)

Gall Bladder 34 (GB 34) "Yang Hill Spring" relieves joint stiffness in the body. It is an "influential" point for the muscles and tendons. These are points that gather or accumulate Qi for a particular region. GB 34 gathers Qi for the tendons and muscles and this allows for a broad effect on these regions. This point is located on the outside of the hind leg just below the stifle (hind leg knee) joint. You will feel two bony prominences there and the point sits in the valley between the two mountains. See image below.

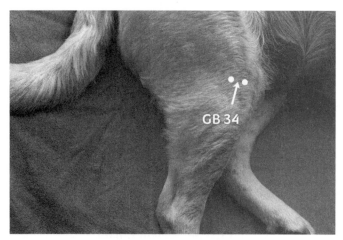

Figure 4: Gall Bladder (GB 34)

4. The Fire Dog

*When tempted to fight fire with fire, remember that
the fire department usually uses water.*
—DANA BARZILAY

"In bursts the second dog, a flash of fiery red..."

Characteristics of a Fire Dog

Everyone adores a Fire Dog! And a Fire Dog loves to be adored. Not only do they thrive on social interactions and attention but they carry a warm charisma and magnetism that is hard to ignore. People and other animals are drawn to the light that Fire Dogs carry. They can even make us feel lighter just by being in their presence.

Fire Dogs are the ones that you will feel staring at you from across the road, just wishing you into looking their way. When you finally do make eye contact, they light up and are super excited that you've noticed them. You find yourself zombie-like drawn to visit them and they reciprocate with wiggles and wags like they've known you forever. Strangely, you feel the same way! Fire Dogs, often red or a red combination, are happy being the center of attention in any crowd. They thrive on play, adoration, and social stimulation. They are the quintessential party dog!

The Fire Dog needs both physical and emotional contact as much as they need food. Fire Dogs are very cuddly. They are as good at giving affection as receiving it. They love fun activities, are quick learners, and fun to train. They love praise and will create lifelong partnerships and friendships with other animals and humans.

Fire Dogs are all about relationship and heart, which is appropriate since the heart is one of the Fire element's main organs, joined by the pericardium, the protector for the heart. Balanced heart-fire energy

Fire Element Dogs

Personality characteristics and support for well-being and balance

Archetype	Party Animal, Diva
Strengths	Charismatic magnetism, friendly, social, playful, fast learner, loves attention and to be adored
Emotional default	Ungrounded, reactivity, disturbance of the Shen
Season	Summer
Organs	Heart, small intestine, pericardium, triple heater
Time	11:00 a.m. – 3:00 p.m. and 7:00 p.m. – 11:00 p.m.
Sense organ	Tongue (licking)
Sense	Speech (barking)
Coat color	Often red or red and white
Common issues	Skin disorders, nervous stomach, heat issues, inflammation
Wants	Play, social stimulation, adoration, cuddles
Needs	Grounded owner, feeling loved, touch, constant emotional connection
Stressors	Overstimulation, busy environments, chaos, being alone or separated from bonded animals or people, heat
Response to stress	Drama queen, stomach upsets, Shen disturbances
Stress support	Physical and emotional contact, attention, fun activities, coolness, soft words and praise, a calm, grounded person or animal
Supportive therapies	Calm touch such as massage and calming acupressure points, cooling foods such as turkey, duck, rabbit, whitefish, cool areas to rest, quiet grounding exercises (ground yourself first!)
Relationship support	Create fun training sessions and be emotionally connected and supportive during training, praise calmly and lavishly! Take them everywhere, especially on your normal routines and walks where they can be adored and feel safe.

can be laser-focused on a passion, providing a gentle warming of the spirit and heart. Or, it can be mildly expansive, inspiring potential, and full of the gifts of light and promise. However, heart-fire imbalances may create too much expansion, and can, in a flash, turn into fear and drama. Being incredibly social and relationship-based, Fire Dogs typically do not like being alone and may insist on going everywhere with you . . . or else!

Think of cuddling up to a cozy campfire on a cool, starlit night while you happily cook your food and listen to the owls hooting and the crickets singing . . . *Aaaaah* . . . Now think of a raging wildfire creating chaos everywhere. *EEEK*!

This can be the emotional span of your Fire Dog!

Best Practices for Working with Fire Dogs

Fire Dogs are extremely sensitive to others as well as their surroundings, and can easily become mentally and emotionally overloaded. This charming, heartfelt, and joyful dog can quickly become a drama queen! In TCM we call this a disturbance of the Shen. The Shen is the combination of the spirit, mind, and body. The Shen is housed in the heart. The heart is a Fire element yin organ with a wide emotional span. This makes it an organ of paradox—one minute we can be feeling terribly sad about something and the next minute we see something beautiful that moves our emotional needle 180 degrees to pure joy. The ensuing Heart Fire from this needle spin can create a state of excess joy. This excess joy can cause the Fire element dog (or human) to be unpredictable, ungrounded, and emotionally reactive, creating dramatic or unsuitable behavior.

At this point, we humans need to support our Fire Dog by remembering to ground ourselves first. This can be accomplished quickly by taking a deep breath and feeling your feet solidly on the ground as you quickly assess the situation that is triggering the disturbance of the Shen.

Next, take the Fire Dog calmly and quietly out of the fray. Then begin to soothe them with some tender touch, acupressure points, and soft words, which should re-ground the wild Heart Fire. Usually, they snap back to their adorable, sweet, party dog self, and life goes on while you are still wondering what just happened.

The Story of Louie

On a lovely beach in Puerto Rico a young, feral street dog, starved, broken, nearly hairless, but with a bright fiery spirit all his own, literally soared into my heart and arms. He smiled a full toothed smile and then growled at me while joyously licking my face. I immediately fell in love with this magnetic, kooky little guy. I was deeply touched by his spirit and quickly fell prey to his joyful Heart Fire and odd charisma. I felt as if I was being reunited with a long-lost friend. Clearly, he did, too!

For some odd reason the name Louie burst out of my mouth as I carefully put him down, still growling and licking. He had followed a group of middle school children that we had taken on a cultural exchange program and had dubbed himself Team Mascot for our two-week visit. As is typical for a Fire Dog, everybody loved him and he loved them. However, Louie made it perfectly clear to the others that the only one who was allowed to touch him was me. I had become "his human." Louie spent the next 17 years going everywhere with me.

Louie was adorable, even half naked, he had the charismatic magnetism of all Fire Dogs and humans. He was a one-year-old border collie/mega-mix/street dog born on the streets of Puerto Rico that had been shot and beaten (resulting in numerous broken bones shown on the x-rays when we got back home to the US) and had missing parts and pieces. But he still possessed a love and zest for life and all things social and fun – on his terms.

As a savvy street dog, Louie was extremely attuned and sensitive to others. He always knew what they were thinking or about to do, even before they did. He had a hair-trigger personality that could be smiley, wiggly, and waggy. But if a hand reached out other than mine, the fierce but quiet Louie lip snarl would scare people out the door. Yet, he was still a magnet for everyone who saw him. Everyone wanted to meet him, touch him, or be near him. It was stunning and absolutely amazing to watch! Strangely enough, he not only tolerated but loved the attention, energetically soaking it up like the cute, hedonistic ham he was. But his rule was "no touch"—me excluded. I can count on one hand the unknowing humans that he allowed to pet him—which would momentarily take my breath away—and it was only one or two soft swipes before the lip-curling, glazed-eye response emerged. The Fire Qi imbalance that that resulted from early trauma followed him around like his tail. His puppyhood troublemaker past had created a deep-seated Shen disturbance which made safe boundaries for him, but not for others.

On Louie's first night home with us, this showed up dramatically at meal time. Cedar, our kind but firm elder female, the very balanced Water/Wood element of our pack, taught me a lesson. Louie began to snarl as I attempted to set down his food bowl. Cedar looked Louie straight in the eye and he stopped snarling. With all her wisdom, she just walked away. In watching this I sensed her leadership, compassion, and empathy for Louie and his past, as did the other dogs watching. It suddenly dawned on me that I should follow Cedar's example and give Louie the space to heal and feel safe. Thanks to Cedar's wisdom, I realized he had earned the right to guard his food while starving on the streets of Puerto Rico. I should just alleviate the meal time stress, do my job, and leave him be. Eventually my Wood element trait of persistence gave up as my primary Water element's deep wisdom and empathy took over. A quick setting down of the bowl became the normal routine for many years to come, with snarling becoming quieter and quieter as the years rolled by. Louie's Shen disturbance was not to be fully altered until much, much later in his life.

Animals of all elements that are injured at a young age have an incredible adaptive resilience. This comes from a sense of "normalcy" in living with the pain of injuries; they simply don't know life any other way. Each element will show that resilience differently. Louie's strong Fire element resilience had amazingly carried him to age 17, with a fiery zest for life that was still going strong until his last days.

Common Ailments in Fire Dogs

Physically, Fire Dogs like Louie may have imbalances from excess heat, both inside and outside their bodies. They may have stomach or gut issues from stress and drama, allergies, itchiness, or skin and shoulder issues. They also may be prone to heart conditions. The heart is one of the key organs of the Fire element and houses the Shen. Keeping them grounded, cool, feeling loved and socially engaged and giving them regular caring, physical touch can keep them balanced for a long, happy and fun life. Most Fire Dogs absolutely love and need touch. Shen-disturbed dogs like Louie are the exceptions, but they will often allow their owners the privilege of safe touch while still desiring the social contact of other humans' hands-off adoration.

Fire Dog Life Lesson
Practice emotional quietness in the midst of drama.

Fire Element Rescue Dogs – Chaos to Connection

Fire Dogs are often the first ones adopted because they carry their charismatic magnetism wherever they go. They are the ones at the kennel door that are just begging for you to notice them, and when you do, they soulfully look deeply into your eyes… and then they've "gotcha!" They are adorable, delightful, and you just want to take them home. When you get to meet them, they snuggle up to you. They feel like a brand-new appendage you suddenly grew. The more you adore them, the more they burrow into you and your heart. You sign the papers and off you go. Fire Dog rides happily in your arms as you head home.

When you get home she jauntily struts in and meets everyone as she wanders about the house with a lively prance, being the social bunny that she is. Everyone adores her, cuddles with her—even the cat likes her—sort of.

Miss Fire Dog gets over-excited with all this attention and starts to chaotically zoom around and run on the furniture, knocking things over and chasing the cat, while panting and looking wide-eyed and stressed. You think it is just because she is out of her shelter cage and in a new house, so you give her a treat. Finally, she stops breathing hard and settles.But this behavior continues to periodically occur, day after day, looking like anxiety attacks and full-blown panic. All beings in the household become agitated, stressed, and worried. The snuggly times stop and the adoration goes out the window. These behaviors become established on both sides, creating a cycle of imbalance for the Fire Dog and the household. She needs more than treats. Fire Dogs need a lot of social stimulus and love. They need connection, which includes touch and positive attention. They need to know they are your number one priority.

They are very smart, quick learners and want to interact with you or someone else almost constantly. Despite their neediness, they will also give back a lot of affection and devotion. They love to snuggle, do playful things to make you laugh, and look deep into your eyes like they are your best friend reading your soul—which they are. They are sweet, precious beings of light and heart. Yet they "unground" easily, which creates this chaotic rise of emotions within them.

When this occurs, it is best to ground yourself by quickly taking a deep breath, feeling your feet on the ground, and quietly moving Fire Dog out of the chaos. Give her soft touch, quiet words, and gentle praise. This is the panacea for her panic and drama. Think of a Hollywood diva that gets so much adoration, social contact, and love that she actually swoons and faints. This behavior is similar to your Fire Dog.

As rescues, these dogs are easily affected by too much stimulus, especially new stimulus. It is up to us to find their tolerance level and honor it. We need to keep ourselves grounded as well. Their high sensitivity level will feel all our feelings. If we are ungrounded, they will start to levitate too. Find ways to socialize them—take them to fun classes and let them interact with other animals. Be mindful of their activity so as to catch any rise towards chaos ahead of time.

Touch them often, adore them, teach them new fun things, and love them back. They will be the brightest stars that you ever had the pleasure to care for. Everyone will remember them fondly for lifetimes to come.

Fire Dog Quiz	
1 = Never true | 2 = Sometimes true | 3 = Always true	
	I love all humans and want to be around them
	I wag my whole body incessantly when someone comes to say hi
	I love to be petted and noticed
	I sometimes have separation anxiety when my human leaves
	I love to be petted and always want more
	I treat everyone like I've known them forever
	I need to feel loved at all times, feeling loved makes me feel safe
	I can be a bit of a ham and want to be adored by everyone
	I'm smart but have trouble focusing for too long when new people or friends are around
	I can get overexcited and turn into a drama queen
	People get happy when they meet me or visit with me
	I enjoy being social with other dogs and want to visit or play with everyone
	When I have too much fun I can panic and get confused
	I overheat easily even when it's not summer
	I can become nervous or full of anxiety if things aren't "normal"
	When I feel stressed I can panic and completely unground
	I can become hypersensitive to foods/lotions/potions and meds
	I bark a lot
	I lick a lot
	I love to cuddle
	Fire Element Dog Total

The Old Fire Dog

Include your Old Fire Dog in your daily life as much as possible. Train them on a ramp early in life so you can load them in the car easily when you run errands. Take short walks about town or in your neighborhood where they can gather attention and feel adored. Have quiet play sessions with other dog friends. Give them cool places to be outside in the summer heat and have regular vet checks for their big hearts. Give them praise for anything and everything!

Louie loved to go to work with me in my truck every day, visiting barns and dog friends, wagging as wildly as his old body would allow when seeing his "no touch" human friends that he loved. He was the perfect gregarious, social partner. People in other cars would often roll down their window and wave at him like the celebrity he thought he was, every stoplight, nearly every day, for 17 years.

One very rainy day we were at a stop light and a limousine pulled up next to us. Louie was sitting upright in the front passenger seat with his window half open. A very well-dressed man and woman rolled down the back window of the limo in the middle of a cloudburst and began waving and talking to him. They were enchanted by him, saying all the perfect sweet goofy words he loved. Louie gave them a few wiggles and smiles. I truly think it made their day. The man looked familiar to me. As the light turned green and they pulled away I saw a government license plate and realized that it was our state governor and his wife adoring my little Louie. He really should have been famous!!

Many celebrity dogs are Fire Dogs. Lassie was a Fire element with Wood (Hero) and Earth (Nurturer). Other examples of famous Fire Dogs are Tramp in Lady and the Tramp, and of course, Snoopy.

In Louie's last years, we called him Galileo because our world revolved around him. His internal clock was still working perfectly. Just as the earth orbits the sun, he knew exactly when breakfast should be, walkies should happen, and when dinner should be served. He was still steadfast and consistent about our rhythms down to the minute. I admired him for that. My own clock would often go astray with distractions, so I happily encouraged him to keep me on time. After all, he had been my timekeeper for nearly 17 years, even reminding me at 8:45 a.m. each Friday, standing on his hind legs looking out the window that overlooked the driveway, that Margaret the housekeeper was on her way. Amazingly, his internal clock also included a calendar; he only did this on Fridays at the prescribed time.

He desperately loved Margaret and as she drove slowly and carefully up the driveway, he danced around her car until she opened the driver's side door. Then he would soar over her into the passenger seat and ride the rest of the way up the drive. He smiled and twirled around her as she walked in the door giggling at his spins and antics. Friday mornings were a regular replay of Mrs. Doubtfire in our house with the two of them happily dancing around my Hoover. He loved the cocktail of stimulus, movement, and her 65-year-old sweetness. Louie was the quintessential Fire element party dog —full of love and joy.

As he aged toward 17, long naps frequently interrupted his liveliness, but once he was awake again, he would always step back into his role as timekeeper and master of our planet called Home. In his last year, Louie's food guarding finally softened. He welcomed me and my spoon scraping the last few bites off the sides of his bowl for him to finish. This change was one of the subtle shifts of him aging, a sense of finally giving in to the help I quietly offered him, and a relinquishing of the past.

Louie's final meal was outdoors, with warm chicken, cheddar cheese, and a cocktail of love, prayers, and letting go. A hail storm with thunder and lightning poured down off the mountain as we lay in a meadow of bright yellow glacier lilies, huddled under a prayer blanket. His friends were there to escort him—a coyote and a small wolf that had been coming to me in my dreams for several weeks to let me know it was Louie's time to meet his companions on the other side. A suitable and colorful send-off for his special Fire element soul!

Remember to spoil your Old Fire Dog lavishly! They deserve it and need it. But most of all, schedule regular time to share touch with them.

This special being has brought smiles and joy into so many other lives and your loving touch is a great way to give them smiles and joy back.

> **Old Fire Dog Life Lesson**
> Carry love in your heart and spread it everywhere, even if it makes you a little crazy sometimes. You will touch many and they will always remember you for it!

Issues for Older Fire Dogs

Stressors: Being alone, left behind, or separated from caregiver, lack of social contact and adoration, heat, lack of fun, chaos, big household changes.

Response to Stress: Nervousness, shaking, depression, drama.

Stress Balancers: Praise them for anything and everything, numerous short "adoration walks," include them in daily life and errands, quiet fun play sessions or games, cool areas for rest, share touch often.

Relationship Support: Stay grounded amidst challenges, stay emotionally and physically connected, and appreciate the joy they give to us and others around them.

Acupressure Points
for the Fire Dog

Please refer to the guidelines for acupressure in Chapter 2, page 34.

> CAUTION: Do not use these points on pregnant animals!

Governing Vessel (GV 29) "Yin Tang" calms the spirit and quiets the mind. It is a powerful calming point and emotion point. It relieves stress, worry, and anxiety. It can be a great session starting point for wiggly or hypervigilant dogs. It is also a communication gateway. This point is located between and just above the eyes where the "eyebrows" would meet; see top image on the next page (Figure 5).

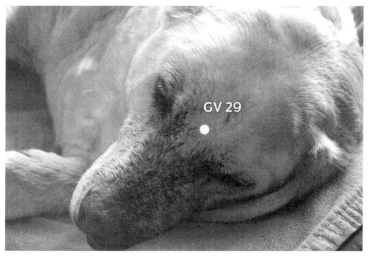

Figure 5: Governing Vessel (GV 29) "Yin Tang"

Pericardium 6 (PC 6) "Inner Gate" is another relaxation point. It's also a useful point for the abdomen and chest. It helps gastrointestinal issues such as nausea, diarrhea, and coughing. It is known as the "sea-sickness" point for humans. PC 6 is located on the inside of the foreleg just above the "wrist" joint of the dog. You will feel a divot just after the bony feel of the joint. See image below.

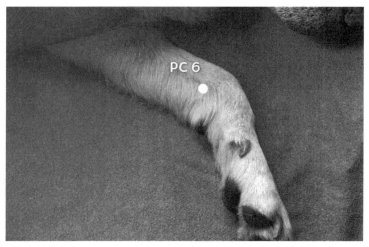

Figure 6: Pericardium 6 (PC 6)

5. The Earth Dog

To sit with a dog on a hillside on a glorious
afternoon is to be back in Eden, where doing
nothing was not boring— it was peace.

—MILAN KUNDERA

"The third dog, a bit pudgy and yellow, looks to his
handler with worried eyes..."

Characteristics of an Earth Dog

Earth Dogs are the quintessential caregivers. Kind, gentle, brave, abundantly patient, and a bit chubby. The perfect kid-loving family dog. Earth Dogs are routine-based by nature and have amazingly accurate internal clocks. They are easy-going, love everyone, love touch, comfort, genuine praise, and of course, food.

As I write this, I'm watching my older rescue Earth Dog, Wilbur, play ever so gently and patiently with my new four-month-old rescue pup Pretzel. They are sharing a dog bed and chew toy and she is singing loudly while Wilbur is gently holding the toy in his mouth and trading it back and forth. They have been playing like this for about four hours. It can be mesmerizing to observe this gentle interplay of kindness and patience between an elder and a puppy.

Pretzel just fell asleep tucked in Wilbur's arms and he hasn't budged, watching over her quietly like the perfect guardian he is. Wilbur, now dubbed "the uncle," has been my best asset with Pretzel, a very sweet, shy, wily, feral Water element dog (more about that mysterious element later). Wilbur has taken on the task of teacher, mentor, and puppysitter. Uncharacteristic for Wilbur, he is now doing everything I ask him to,

Earth Element Dogs

Personality characteristics and support for well-being and balance

Archetype	Quintessential caregiver and nurturer
Strengths	Kind, gentle but brave spirit, patient, loves everyone, loves touch and comfort, dependable, generous, kid-loving, forgiving, great memory, needs routine, with very accurate internal clock
Emotional default	Worry and obsession
Season	Late summer
Organs	Stomach/spleen/pancreas
Time	7:00 a.m. – 11:00 a.m.
Sense organ	Mouth
Sense	Taste
Coat color	Often yellow, tan, or cream or any color that looks chubby
Common issues	Digestive upset, dental issues, growths and fatty tumors, weight gain, gas, bad breath, stifle injuries, hind-end weakness due to weight
Wants	Food, connection, comfort, praise, recognition, love, family
Needs	Routine-based lifestyle, touch, peaceful home atmosphere, food!
Stressors	Lack of routine, complicated requests, expectations of mental quickness
Response to stress	Worry, stubbornness, obsessiveness, lack of confidence, apathy
Stress balancers	Touch, sincere praise, slow fun activities, peaceful environment, comfort, animal and children buddies, weight management
Supportive therapies	Touch, diet considerations, low household stress, regular routine of exercise, herbs or enzymes for digestion, belly lifts for strengthening the back, massage, family, LOVE
Relationship support	Be supportive and patient with slow and steady steps towards a lifetime of dependability and love

while acting like a tour guide of household etiquette. This is the first time I've seen Wilbur willingly comply with house rules. Fortunately, Pretzel is extremely visual and smart, and is learning to mimic his oddly perfect behavior. He has even helped me potty train her by going potty on command every single time I ask! He is happily living his Earth element with purpose and patience.

Earth is the center of all life. It is supportive in every way. It supports the roots and growth of billions of trees, plants, and people. It creates the promise of Fire and sustenance. Earth holds Water and creates flow and places of deep calmness, holding space for many ancient creatures, giving life to all inhabitants. Earth provides us with fresh air to breath and precious metals to create, innovate, and admire. Earth holds community. Everything comes from the support of Earth.

Earth element dogs are the unsung heroes of the dog world. They are always there for us—supportive, hardworking, courageous, patient, caring, and nurturing. They give us the love of necessity, the deep love of a mother, a caregiver. They treat everyone like family, and worry and care deeply for the well-being of others regardless of race, gender, or species. They happily wag their tails for all and gently protect those who need it. They are nourishment and love. They embrace community. They are Earth in a furry body.

Earth Dogs have an abundance of patience which can be laced with quiet determination when they want something. This is a polite way of saying that stubbornness and obsessiveness can be two of their shadow traits. I have found that there is a fine line between patience and stubbornness, and it all depends on our chosen human perspective.

Earth Dogs are not always quick, complex thinkers. It takes patience and a lot of treats to teach them, so short, quick lessons are best. However, their memory is excellent and once they learn and master something, they will never forget it.

The Earth Element Dog's learning style echoes our Planet Earth, as it should. Earth carries its memories and records from its inception to current day, surprising us with new discoveries of ancient life and learning all the time. Earth Dogs, although seemingly slow to learn sometimes, will surprise you months or years later by perfectly completing a task or request you tried to train into them and gave up on. Their storage capacity is just different, more akin to Planet Earth. Like Earth, these dogs hold deep, important memories and teachings and release them when the time is right. That clearly shows a strong type of intelligence—an intelligence of prioritizing other Earth Element aspects such as devotion and nurturing over short-term recall. Short-term recall is best achieved with an Earth Dog by having a whole pocket full of treats! Who is teaching who? Isn't it quite intelligent how they are actually training us?!

Our celebrity Earth Dogs… Benji, Enzo, Marley, Scooby Doo, and Old Yeller.

The Story of Wilbur

Wilbur came to me in a dream—three vivid lucid dreams, actually—my first dreams in seven months, after a severe head and spinal injury caused by a horse, that changed my life. Six days after the injury, I had lost my sweet older Water Dog Luna following a long, hard bout with an aggressive tumor. I was dogless for the first time in 40 years, and if I ever needed a dog to give me courage and a will to heal, it was then.

As soon as I was able, I began searching for a dog on the internet. It was summer of 2020 and the pandemic was raging across the country. Everyone was working from home and adopting dogs like crazy. As soon as a young dog came up on an adoption site, it was gone. Forlorn and lonely, I kept trying, while visualizing daily to manifest "my best dog ever"—a tall order as I have lived with so many amazing ones. I said many prayers asking Creator to help me out.

One night, in my dreams, a mature yellow lab male appeared, saying he would be here soon to help. I told him I was looking for a puppy, but he persisted, dream after dream. As a healer, I have a lot of animals visit me in my dreams, some passing through to the Beyond, some just wondering when I'm coming back to see them (their mom usually calls the next day), and some just visiting to thank me for helping them. This was different—purposeful and aimed right at my heart. This yellow lab was for real, and I somehow knew that.

The morning after the last of the three dreams, I was on the phone consulting for a Texas horse and dog rescue center and jokingly asked if they had a yellow lab puppy. No, she said, but we have six-year-old Wilbur! Wilbur was picked up by the rescue that same morning, the day he was slated to be euthanized by a kill shelter. He had been turned in to the shelter by a disheveled, broken man, Wilbur's former owner, who could no longer care for him. Wilbur then made the crazy long trek from Texas to the Pacific Northwest with 34 rescued chihuahuas in a van. The harried and weary yellow lab from my dream was here.

Wilbur arrived nearly hairless, very ill, wild-eyed with worry, and almost unmanageable. He had clearly been extracted from a life of love, fun, and family. He whined, wagged, and cried when he saw a young child or a teenage boy, as if searching for the family he left behind. Yet under all that chaos was a kind, gentle nature, a sweet, loving family dog that had been traumatized by the stress of change. Our wounds immediately bonded us, our sorrows, our major life changes, our broken hearts. Considering my injury, physical condition, and emotional state, it was not surprising that a nurturing Earth element dog came to my rescue.

Recognizing him as an Earth Dog, I found my purpose and partner again in facilitating healing for both of us. In that purpose, we healed each other. I stabilized routines for him, gave him oodles of praise for the smallest things, let him help me when I needed it, and of course made sure there were plenty of "Earth Dog security snacks" to re-channel his worry and obsessiveness, and in return he gave me pure devotion, laughter, purpose to move when it was hard, gentle kindness, snuggly protection, and a loving presence that is hard to describe but I'll try...

When one is wounded deeply in body, mind, heart, and spirit, having a kindred, knowing, furry being watch over you, protect you, hold your tears, wag when you need it most and just be there when you need someone, is a profound gift. Wilbur is brave, strong, and gentle, and carries that presence with grace, ease, and a little chubbiness… just like an Earth element should.

Best Practices for Working
with Earth Dogs

Earth Dogs love and need praise and recognition, but they love FOOD even more. They are major foodies. If you lengthen lessons when training or ask too much, they can become stubborn, not just a little stubborn, but persistently stubborn! High value treats like bacon can definitely extend the lesson time, but there will come a point when the Earth Dog's mental clock and interest runs out, usually just about the same time as your treats do!

Earth Dogs are "easy keepers." In other words, they gain weight just by looking at food. Food is one of their greatest motivators in life, so it is important to watch what and how much you feed them. Be sure to count their treats into your calorie count. No fun, I know. Don't fret though—regular exercise and possibly a new puppy will help a little bit with their propensity for chubbiness.

Earth Dogs have exceptional internal clocks and will always remind you if you are late for a meal or a walk. To an Earth Dog, walkies are not as interesting as meals, but they will still keep you on track because there may be treats involved. Earth Dogs are very "routine-based" and will always do best with regular routines. This gives them a sense of security.

Common Ailments in Earth Dogs

The emotion associated with the Earth element is worry. Any form of change or household imbalance (new puppy, packing a suitcase, late dinner, stressful conversations, a household move) tips them into worry. This intense worry can create stomach issues causing all sorts of digestive upsets. Having an awareness and understanding of their propensity for worry goes a long way towards keeping them balanced and healthy, especially in the elder Earth Dog. Earth Dogs can also have hind leg issues, fatty tumors, and other growths. Their metabolisms tend to be a little slower, so adding doggie digestive enzymes into their daily food is a big help. This should be a regular practice for the elder Earth Dog and helpful for younger Earth Dogs too. If you see or feel lumps or bumps on their body consult your veterinarian.

The Story of Wilbur, Part 2

Wilbur loves scent work and is amazing at it, mostly because food is involved. Scent work is one time when leash pulling and obsessiveness is actually a good thing! Pull mom around, find the hide, get the treats! An Earth element dog's dream. Wilbur is sharp, quick, and fast. He is fearless with complete body confidence to go in, under, or on top of anything to uncover the hide. Obsessive? Yes! Even in the water as we swim he scents a diving duck and tracks it by scent from above while it is still under water.

One Sunday morning my husband Mark had the hood of our car open trying to locate a rather stinky mouse nest. (Our home is surrounded by a 740-acre forested land trust and that means a lot of mice.) We'd had Wilbur only a few months; he was still decompressing from the change and we were still learning about him. Turns out he was and still is, an avid and persistent mouse hunter.

He stood on two legs at the front wheel of the car and glued his nose to one spot, furiously wagging his tail. Mark did not believe there could possibly be a mouse in that particular spot and ignored Wilbur's insistent and determined "alert." (An alert is a term we use in scent work that is a signal the dog gives when he has found his target.) After nearly an hour of Wilbur persistently standing on two legs (patient...obsessive or both?), furiously wagging his tail in a particularly unusual way (his alert), I offered Mark my favorite saying that I learned from numerous scent and search and rescue dogs: Always trust your dog.

Mark looked a little deeper and then saw the nest in the corner of the open car hood, right under Wilbur's nose. It was packed with fuzzy mouse nesting material and a stockpile of yummy mouse treats for her brood-to-be who could be arriving any minute. Momma was hiding in a deep, dark corner and she and her cozy nest went on a carefully designed relocation program.

Sometimes Earth Dog obsessiveness is a good thing!

In the few years we've had him, Wilbur has managed to make many friends. He is the Grand Greeter. Like the Fire Dog, he attracts people, but for a different reason. It is not magnetic charisma, but his gentleness and friendliness that reels them in. Everyone who walks by my car or we see on the trails has to greet Wilbur. This creates all sorts of magical conversations that would never have happened if it weren't for his full-bodied smile and wildly wagging tail. Embrace the Earth Dog's slower pace and gentle, friendly spirit and it will open up your world.

> **Earth Dog Life Lesson**
> Slow down, be grateful, and notice gentleness. Be friendly!

Earth Element Rescue Dogs –
Eat, Play, Nap, Love

Earth Dog rescues are wonderful! They are friendly, open-hearted beings that will catch your attention in the shelter. When they see you approaching the kennel they will show their best smiley face and wag, wag, wag. If you look closely you will see a veiled look of worry in their eyes, worry that you might not take them home.

Most of the time when the Earth Dog finds the right home and settles in, they are incredibly happy, nurturing, and loving. During this settle-in time you may notice bouts of worry from your rescue Earth Dog. Support these with kindness and loving touch. Belly rubs are usually their favorite or just some soft, calming ear rubs will often do wonders. Sometimes just spending a few moments cuddling and being close to them is all it takes for reassurance. If you give treats for every worry session, you will just have more worry sessions. That falls into the category of who is training who? Instead notice, give praise, and some gentle, supportive touch and then redirect him to something interesting or fun like his new toy or going outside for a walk. These dogs can be masters at finding creative ways to beg and acquire food, so treats are not the answer to their woes. Also remember the stressors for Earth Dogs; packing things up, loneliness, loud tense voices all add up to worry for them. They are family-oriented dogs and devoted to their children, animal friends, and human partners. They are social, love to greet everyone with wiggles and joy, and love visitors on their home turf. They like the slow life and enjoy relaxing with their humans and friends. They provide a quiet and vigilant protection over their family, hard to notice until it is needed. They need a regular rhythmic lifestyle as they have perfectly timed clocks and large-capacity tummies that love food. Earth Dogs are loving, generous, low maintenance, and connect with us in a deep, comfortable, and soulful way. They are solid, faithful friends through the storms of life.

Earth Dogs are trustworthy, sensitive, fun, caring, generous, and kind. They are also worriers. Worry is their default stress reflex. Because they are extremely devoted to their humans, home, and family, when separated from them for too long or forever, intense worry sets in. This reflex can sometimes show itself with obsessiveness and stubbornness under certain circumstances such as a change of home life.

When you bring your Earth Dog home they will act happy but may easily slip into worry, even though they are eternally grateful to be out of the kennel and may immediately love who you are. They are quiet worriers to start with, but if you look closely, you can see it in their eyes. They very much live in the now. An unknown venue or future can create insecurity. They are not fast learners but hold deep memory capacity for home and the humans of their past life. They will often see someone that may look like a former family member or friend and get overwhelmingly needy and stressed. It's sad to see a heart so big be so sad.

Time, treats, consistency, and your continued affection and praise for even little things will settle the Earth Dog's gentle heart and create some peace to replace their concern. Spending time just sitting together, snuggling, and being proud of who they are is the best medicine for a rehomed Earth Dog. There will always be a safe harbor for you in their heart.

Earth Dog Quiz
1 = Never true | 2 = Sometimes true | 3 = Always true
I love having children or other pets around me
I love meeting new people
I am very loyal to my family
I love having company visit, both animals and humans
I get very worried when things change in my household
I worry and obsess when my food is late
I do not like suitcases
I get confused with too much training or too many requests
I never forget a face or place
I protect my family especially the little ones
I sashay when I walk while my tail wags a lot
I love quiet time with my special person
I LOVE TREATS and ask for them regularly
I get very stressed and go flat and hide when people argue or yell
I love to snuggle with anyone and everyone
I'm not very competitive
I share my toys and bed
I take on my human's stress
I can be overprotective
I gain weight easily
Earth Element Dog Total

The Old Earth Dog

The Old Earth Dog needs comfort and a peaceful atmosphere with very little change and the same routine-based lifestyle tailored to his age requirements. They always need a lot of praise for doing small things; it makes them feel loved. Old Earth Dogs like to have buddies with them. Cats, other dogs, and children feed their nurturing spirit. They also need to keep an adequate weight for the age-related decrease in physical exercise and metabolism. Chubbiness will be a detriment to them as they age. Feeding them vegetables when they are young so they learn to like them early, is a good, sneaky, low-calorie way to help fill the tummy.

Old Earth Dogs like the slow life so getting them to exercise may take some gentle prodding and praise. Because they love routine, you can keep the same exercise routine and timeframes as in their younger years. Just dial it back a bit; they will do their best to get motivated. Be sure to find "low calorie" treats for the motivation factor. More frequent walks with shorter duration are best for Old Earth Dogs and all older dogs. Their bodies can't handle the long walks of days past; however, frequent short walks are very beneficial to our furry seniors especially those with arthritis. Getting out in the fresh air is actually very important for all dogs. Being cooped up in the cozy house sounds nice but the reality is it dulls their tired old senses. To slow down cognitive decline their senses need stimulus from nature's smells, sounds, and the active visual movements of trees, birds, bugs, cars, people, in the everchanging atmosphere of the great outdoors. Even a small backyard works wonders. Many older dogs love being outside, just being part of the landscape. And they love it even more when we join them. Enjoying the gentle stimulus of smells, sights, and sounds, is good medicine for us all.

Also allow them time for Earthing. Earthing is best done with a full belly on a warm sunny day stretched out on his side next to his human or cat friend with a big dog smile on his face. Blending with the rhythms of the Earth is vital to an Old Earth Dog's well-being and passage home.

Old Earth Dogs really need their humans to spend time just being with them. Outside is best, while giving them long, loving belly rubs and frequent petting. Earth Dogs crave touch. Some of the best memories I have with my Old Dogs is taking the time to simply sit and just be with them. It is a profound and loving gesture in dog language and a healing balm for our own hearts.

> **Old Earth Dog Life Lesson**
> Sometimes the solidness, consistency, and trust in the same old thing can remove worry and allow our hearts to give and receive more love, support, and smiles in our daily routines. Reciprocity at its best!

Issues for Older Earth Dogs

Old Earth Dog Stressors: Being alone or separated from their family members, lack of routine, household changes or stress, inconsistency in feeding times.

Response to Stress: Worry, digestive upsets, obsessive cognitive behavior, depression.

Stress Balancers: Spend quiet time with them doing nothing, belly rubs, Earthing, maintain feeding and exercise on a regular routine, offer healthy low-calorie treats, praise for every effort to exercise or move as they age, surround with family both furry and human.

Relationship Support: Eliminate or mitigate any potential situations for worry, appreciate and support his gentleness and friendliness and give that back always, spend quiet time with him daily, be routinely consistent with this and all his aging needs, train him early with ramps and slings so he will allow help when he needs it.

Acupressure Points
for the Earth Dog

Please refer to the guidelines for acupressure in Chapter 2, page 34.

CAUTION: Do not use these points on pregnant animals!

Stomach 36 (ST 36) "Foot Three Mile" is a master point for the gastro-intestinal tract. It can stimulate appetite and is a whole-body energizer. It wakes up the body! It strengthens Qi, strengthens the immune system, and boosts natural energy. ST 36 has many varied functions depending on what it is paired with and is used in many acupoint recipes. It is the "everything" point, like salt in cooking.

This point is located on the outside of the hind leg just below the stifle (hind leg knee) joint. Slide up in between the outside and front of the leg and just before you feel the bone ST 36 will be the dip/divot in the muscle tissue. This point can be hard to locate on some animals. If you have trouble finding it, just move up and down, gently rubbing in the general area and you will indirectly stimulate the point. Most dogs love having this area rubbed. See image below.

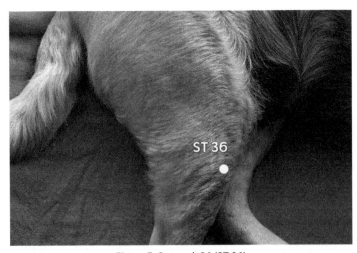

Figure 7: Stomach 36 (ST 36)

Spleen 6 (SP 6) "Three Yin Meeting" is a master point that works with the three yin channels of the spleen, kidney, and liver. It helps relieve fatigue or weakness, helps with GI issues, and is helpful for chronic diarrhea in dogs. It is also used for allergic or immune-related issues. It's located just above the hock, on the back inside of the hind leg. Feel for the back of the long bone above the hock and follow it up 1/4 of the way up to the stifle (hind leg knee). See image below.

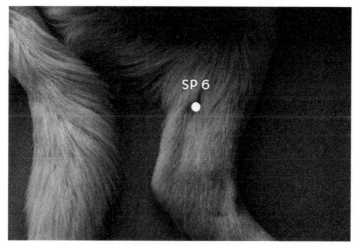

Figure 8: Spleen 6 (SP 6)

6. The Metal Dog

If we take good care of ourselves, we help everyone. We stop being a source of suffering to the world and we become a reservoir of joy and freshness.
—THICH NHAT HANH

"*The fourth dog is lean, angular, greyish tan, and walks quietly . . .*"

Characteristics of a Metal Dog

We often describe the Metal element archetype as a librarian. Extremely intelligent, methodical, calm with a clear mind, dependable, a solid working sense, devoted to a purpose yet deeply sensitive and easily rattled by noise and lack of order. Generally, not desiring or very tolerant of emotional or physical closeness. This is the Metal Dog.

The Energy of Metal is secretive. It is like air. Mutable and yet essential. This profound element is relentlessly curious, diverse, and with diligence, can be shaped. Metal is birthed in the earth. It holds tremendous knowledge but doesn't always share its secrets unless we are able to "unearth" its strength, purposeful vision, and clear ingenuity. To perform, Metal requires earnest and clear intention, and consistent trust. Flexibility does not come easily. Metal must be tempered with extremes: it dances with Fire, creates and holds Water, chops Wood, and hides in Earth.

Best Practices for Working with Metal Dogs

Metal Dogs are capable of intense focus and are mentally and physically competent. They like challenges and doing things that matter. Metal Dogs thrive on having a sense of purpose and having a handler that

Metal Element Dogs

Personality characteristics and support for well-being and balance

Archetype	The Librarian
Strengths	Extremely intelligent, methodical, sensitive, clear-minded focus
Emotional default	Grief
Season	Autumn
Organs	Lung and large intestine
Time	3:00 a.m. – 7:00 a.m.
Sense organ	Nose
Sense	Smell
Coat color	Often grey, white, tan, or rusty, and lean and muscular
Common issues	Skin, respiratory and leg issues, constipation, immune issues
Wants	To work, to have a purpose, to be respected, to trust handler
Needs	Work, purpose, quiet and calm atmosphere for both work and recovery, clear and concise training and communication
Stressors	Commotion, noise, sentimentality, touch, loss of a bonded handler or animal or job
Response to stress	Internalizes stress, impatience, irritation, grief, emotional withdrawal, coughing, skin issues, physical, mental, and emotional rigidity
Stress balancers	Quiet time alone, routine, work, a fully present handler or partner
Supportive therapies	Often does not desire touch but in time can be coaxed to accept it, including acupressure or energy work. Quiet space to recover without noise or chaos. Doggie yoga for flexibility.
Relationship support	Earn his respect and trust by being clear and competent with your training and direction. Bonds deeply to a person he trusts and respects, and will be extremely loyal.

takes their partnership seriously. They bond deeply with their handlers once they can trust that the person is fully present, competent, and committed to their training. They make incredible working dogs as they have a calm and cool exterior, yet a strong inner sensitivity.

Due to this strong sensitivity, they do not tolerate long-term noisy, chaotic atmospheres. They will internalize the stress of the chaos, which creates imbalance and ultimately taxes their well-being and health. They do not need much social interaction, but rely on the few trusted deep bonds they make in their world at home and "work." Metal Dogs can be very focused competitors and often are happiest as working dogs. They typically do not enjoy or need touch, but with trust and time can learn to accept it. Metal Dogs always need to have a quiet place to escape and rejuvenate after giving their all.

The Story of Jack

One morning I was heading into a barn for treatments and noticed a strange-looking white object sticking out of a hole at the entrance. As I got closer I saw a small brown and white tail wiggling wildly next to what appeared to be a leg cast with little swollen toes sticking out. There was no indication of any other body parts, but clearly whoever was down there was still alive, as told by the wagging tail.

I asked the barn manager about the little being in the hole. I suspected it was her Jack Russell terrier Jack. I knew he was an A class rat hunter and part of the "Jack pack" she brought to work each day. She told me that Jack had been stepped on by a horse a few days earlier and had his leg set in a cast. Now he was back at his sole purpose in life—hunting for rats. I knew Jack; he was a very strong Metal element, purposeful, devoted to his barn-clearing job, did not really need or want to be petted or handled, and took serious naps in between his hardworking daytime gig as "head ratter" at the barn.

Jack was the classic Metal. Intelligent, head and body literally buried in his work, methodical in his actions, pure to his focused breed type and temperament, emotion barely showing in a quiet, undiscernible way, and unequivocally focused on hunting the object of his desire—the rat.

Metal Dogs and Metal humans will be very devoted to their people and their work. Once they establish trust with a partner they bond deeply. If or when that trust is breached, ties may be completely severed, to the point of being irreparable. Metal elements lean towards the emotion of grief with any life losses or relationship changes, and this can create a hesitance to trust again. Trust can be hard won with a strong Metal element and their potential for rigidity and lack of flexibility can be high due to this self-protective nature. It may take many attempts at rebuilding the bridge of trust with this intelligent being. Their memory banks are vast and their tolerance for untrustworthy humans low. Once true long-term trust is established they are devoted partners and driven to do their best right alongside you.

The Story of Sage

Sage was a yellow lab mix puppy that also came to me in a dream. In the dream, she told me her name and asked me loud and clear to please come and get her out of her cage. In the dream she was in what looked like an animal shelter.

I was at a seminar with my husband at the time. He had just lost his bloodhound/Australian shepherd mix, K.C. at age fifteen. His heart was sore and tender. Sometimes, the only thing to repair the loss of a beloved dog is another beloved dog. We were staying at a hotel and the next morning I went to the front desk to ask if there was an animal shelter nearby. I was told it was just one block away. I talked my husband into stopping on our way out of town and there she was, little Sage, the puppy from my dream.

I recognized her instantly and she recognized me, responding immediately to her name. We lovingly packed Sage in the car and off we went. Sage was a smart little thing and resourceful, a wee bit feral and yet very devoted to our existing pack family. She was a purposeful, smart Metal element, quietly introverted. However, she also had a strong second Fire element and third Earth element which both required having the comfort and stimulation of family and friends around her at all times. That quickly became apparent as she had a terrible problem with separation anxiety. She had initially bonded with me and would chew anything that I had touched before leaving for work. One sad morning it was the toilet seat!

My husband's grief over losing his last dog kept him from bonding with her. He was a new middle school teacher and was working long days. I had two other dogs going to work with me each day and did not have enough time or energy to take puppy Sage, so she stayed home with uncle dog Riley for the first month.

After the toilet seat massacre, several eviscerated pillows, two disemboweled plants, and a family discussion, she proudly went to school with her dad and their bond was formed. She was the most perfect and cute pup and all the school staff and students fell in love with her sweet, sociable Fire element side. Her Earth element formed deep lasting bonds with many. Her primary Metal made her the star of the school as an unofficial service dog and Sage was quickly recruited to work in the library for Reading with Rover time (before there was such a thing). She spent her days in my husband's classroom as well as other classrooms, a vigilant mascot for signaling physical and emotional issues in children while also providing a calming Earth element touchstone for little hands and hearts when needed.

In a few years this included Sage taking the special needs children for walks when they needed a friend or any emotional assistance. Turns out she had a knack for signaling epileptic seizures in the classrooms and had a gentle, calming influence on ADHD and anxiety-ridden children. She just knew who needed what and when.

Even in our home pack life, she always took the Metal/Earth role of nurse and often alerted me to issues with the other animals, showing me exactly where in their bodies they needed care. She also became mascot of the surf team, spending early mornings on the beach carefully counting heads in the water and notifying my husband the coach if someone was having a hard time out there. Sage had an amazing working dog career for thirteen years. Then her Fire/Metal element dad retired from teaching and both he and Sage flopped into a slump. With the loss of her job and the emotional withdrawal of my husband, she too became apathetic, bored, and depressed. Her grief was palpable. Sage began to develop a slow-growing tumor on her nose which eventually affected her breathing, exactly where she had been bitten by a rattlesnake when she was three years old.

At the time, I had a precocious and highly intelligent Labrador-cross pup named Luna (also known as the "tiny terrorist") who needed a job. Luna had an excellent working mind and was an amazing scent dog so I put her in a nose work class in preparation for doing search and rescue work with me. One day, I had Sage in the car with us as we were arriving at Luna's nose work class. Our instructor Georgia, a retired oncologist turned nose work instructor, immediately spotted Sage's tumor and her obvious apathy. We talked about Sage's amazing life adventures and her current depression, and Georgia invited Sage in to do some nose work. Sage loved it! Finding biscuits hidden in boxes and cubbies, what could be better? This fun work brought her out of her doldrums and she lived two more years, to the ripe old age of fifteen.

Sage's last service work was a month before she passed. She and I were asked to do a nose work demonstration with Georgia, hosted by the American Cancer Society. The ACS's goal was to show that there can still be ways to have fun during life with cancer, even for our animals. Sage, wearing a pink bandanna, pink harness, pink leash, and her now large pink facial tumor, raced through the boxes, finding the scents in record time. The crowd roared! What a sweet "Shero" she was. She left her mark on so many hearts, right up to the end.

Common Ailments in Metal Dogs

The Metal Dog's emotional reflex is grief, and when there is the loss or absence of a bonded handler, companion animal, or even a job they love, they will internalize grief. If there is lack of trust or disconnection with their handler they will withdraw emotionally and shut down. When Metal Dogs internalize their stress, the resulting imbalance can cause respiratory issues, skin troubles, constipation, and immune problems.

Just like metal hidden deep in the earth, this hard-driving, intelligent, and talented dog has deep sensitivity needs that are often hidden from many owners. If you suspect you have a Metal Dog, take some time to truly pay attention to their emotional sensitivities and reshape any imbalances that may occur.

Metal Dogs can also have rigidity issues or lack of flexibility in both their personality and body. They give 110% physically when they work or compete and can acquire leg injuries due to their own personal high-performance standards.

Take the time to truly connect with your Metal Dog, develop two-way trust, know what is under the surface of their purposeful exterior, and support them for their unique and sensitive needs. You and the world around them will be touched and rewarded many times over.

Metal element celebrity dog: none other than Dorothy's Toto!

Metal Dog Life Lesson
Do your best to be competent and committed to your Metal Dog's training, respect her definition of bonding, and be sensitive and tuned in to this hard-working, loyal dog's needs.

Metal Element Rescue Dogs – Hiding in the Light

A Metal Dog will often be seen in the back of the kennel, sometimes coming forward but making little or no eye contact. They look like they are impatiently calculating a way out. Metal Dogs are highly intelligent, do not initially trust easily, are highly sensitive, and can lack emotional and physical flexibility. They do not always appreciate touch and can be a bit aloof with strangers. So, your rescue "meet and greet" may be short and cordial with a tone of "come on, let's get out of here!"

Metal Dogs are, however, amazing partners. Once trust is established, they are fully devoted to the framework of you and them—as long as you pay attention to their needs and wants, particularly in the learning department, both training-wise and experientially. They have a solid working dog temperament, and love to have a purpose in life and a purposeful partner to share it with.

They give their all and often need to hide away or hole up somewhere quiet to rest and recover. They are highly sensitive. External noise and chaos, builds up stress in them and increases their need for hiding when their work is done. This is their way of decompressing and recuperating.

Establishing and maintaining trust in Metal Dogs is important for the relationship. Depending on their former life circumstances, this may take some time. But once it is in place, it is rock-solid unless you really mess up. They will forgive but their brilliant mind will never forget.

Being of the working dog mindset, they do best by going everywhere with you. They are not very good home-bodies. They like to feel the wings of purpose under them, taking them on adventures that mean something, even if that means taking them to your office each day or running errands with them. Like the Wood Dogs, they really need a job and do best when channeling their extreme intelligence, high sensitivity, and spirit for adventure into something meaningful.

A Metal Dog's nose is their main sense. They do great with scent work in any format. Even scent work classes can satisfy their purposeful working dog spirit. They also are the "canaries in the coal mine," and will be extremely sensitive to toxins in the environment. It's important to hear their messages, they are true to their honor.

As rescue recipients we never really know why these dogs get tossed into the system. Understanding their needs ahead of time can provide a solid foundation for a lifetime of partnership and purpose.

Metal Dog Quiz	
1 = Never true | 2 = Sometimes true | 3 = Always true	
	With a competent, correct, and fair handler I am intelligent and a fast learner
	I learn best with a systematic approach
	I avoid conflict
	I am polite around people and other dogs
	I can be stand-offish with both dogs and humans
	I don't really need touch and cuddles
	I don't get overly excited about things in my environment
	I am pretty quiet and don't bark very often
	I tend to be lean and graze my food
	I glide when I walk or run and have good dog posture
	I don't really act crazy or have fun like other dogs
	I love and need to have a purpose
	I grieve when I lose a friend, a job, or one of my people
	I prefer one-on-one relationships
	I don't often play with toys
	I follow all house rules
	I am very patient
	I isolate myself for rest time
	I don't like chaos
	It takes me time to trust someone
	Metal Element Dog Total

The Old Metal Dog

The Old Metal Dog still needs a purpose and mental stimulation. This can be challenging for owners to find. Teaching scent work at a young age or even early in the aging process can give them a fun, rewarding, and purposeful challenge in their later years. The Metal Dog's natural elemental sense is smell so they typically excel at nose work. I've taken many of my aging dogs to canine nose work classes and it has been great enrichment for them. For the Metal Dog, it becomes a purposeful challenge. Some Metal working dogs may have already had this earlier training and will still find it fun and exciting later in life.

Nose work and movement can also strengthen their sensitive respiratory system and keep the body somewhat supple and limber, as can doggie yoga. Nearly all my dogs have vicariously learned to do doggie yoga as I am doing yoga or stretching. They recognize my clear, quiet, and focused energy and inhabit that space along with me as I stretch and breathe. It's a special group bubble of joy and release!

For Old Metal Dogs, as with all dogs, it is important to pay attention to environmental factors affecting their respiratory and immune systems. Their powerful nose may be the only sense they are relying on in their later years. They can be adversely affected and confused by strong scents in detergents and cleaners, carpets, heavy dust loads, smoke, and pest or weed control products, etc. Be safe and green in and around your homes. You have an intelligent, sensitive "sentinel" to remind you to have a healthy household.

Old Metal Dog Life Lesson

When you are overstimulated by all the complexities and details of life, find a quiet place to rest and take a nap. Your sense of purpose will be renewed and your brain, body, and spirit, will thank you.

Issues for Older Metal Dogs

Old Metal Dog Stressors: Lack of order and quiet in the household, boredom, no purpose, no job.

Response to Stressors: Grief, emotional withdrawal, stiffness, body tension sometimes causing tremors.

Stress Balancers: Calm atmosphere, quiet place to rest, downgrade work requirements but give him a job, mental stimulus with games, take him everywhere with you.

Relationship Support: Continue to be clear, quiet, and respectful and don't over-sentimentalize your reactions to his aging. Respect his way of bonding and his way of slowing down. His loyalty, inner sensitivity, intelligence, and independent nature will guide you in his care.

Acupressure Points
for the Metal Dog

Please refer to the guidelines for acupressure in Chapter 2, page 34.

CAUTION: Do not use these points on pregnant animals!

Large Intestine 4 (LI 4) "Joining Valley" is a powerful point for pain and conditions of the front half of the body including the head, eyes, teeth, jaw, neck, ear, shoulder, respiratory system, and large and small intestines. It is commonly known as the "headache point" in the human world, located within the web between your thumb and forefinger. You may find this point is tender. Squeeze it gently with the thumb and forefinger of your opposite hand and you will find some relief. It is known as an elimination point and can help with constipation but should not be used on dogs with, or prone to, diarrhea. It is located underneath the dewclaw on the inside of the dog's front leg. If the dog does not have a dewclaw, feel for the bony bump where the dewclaw should be and drop into the divot slightly forward (towards the toes) of the bony prominence. Be very gentle, this point can be tender to touch. See top image on the next page (Figure 9).

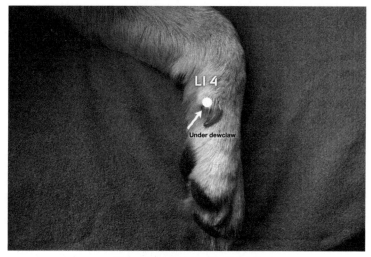

Figure 9: Large Intestine 4 (LI 4)

Lung 9 (LU 9) "Great Abyss" helps clear the lungs of congestion, helps with breathing difficulties, and tonifies the entire respiratory system. It also relieves elbow and shoulder pain. It is located just above LI 4 in what is often called the wrist joint. Slide up to from LI 4 on the inside of the front leg and find the divot in the lower bony area (toward the toes) of the (wrist) joint. See image below.

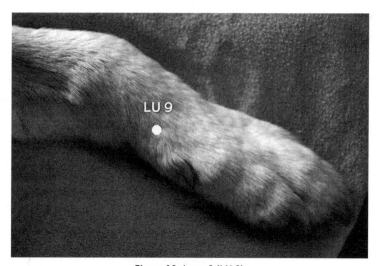

Figure 10: Lung 9 (LU 9)

7. The Water Dog

If there is magic on this planet,
it is contained in water.
—LOREN EISELEY

"The fifth dog, mostly black with a long back,
comes in slowly and quietly…"

Characteristics of a Water Dog

The magical force of the ocean is deep, full of intelligence, teaming with wisdom, unpredictable, and loaded with treasures. So is your Water element dog. When you are ready for one, they come to you and you stand astonished at the complexity of this animal in your life.

Water Dogs teach us to trust in very unconventional ways. We learn trust for them, for ourselves, and for our own inner wisdom. It may not be in the easiest way, but a journey awaits that will enrich, change, and sometimes baffle you. Water Dogs are often considered "a spiritual teacher with four legs."

Water is the source of all life; it nourishes everything and everyone without judgement. It has the quiet, enduring power to transform things that are hard or need shaping. Water feeds Wood, calms Fire, moves Earth, and tempers and strengthens Metal. These qualities make our Water Dogs and Water humans vital to our growth. Through their gentle and often subtle teachings we can make pivotal changes in how we walk in the world. It is in Water's stillness that they access connection to their ancestral wisdom. This nurturing wisdom helps Water Dogs find and ultimately guide their human soul partner to a better way of being.

One way you know you have a Water Dog is that she will show you any of the five elements at any given time. Just as in nature, water has the

Water Element Dogs

Personality characteristics and support for well-being and balance

Archetype	The Empathic One (four-legged spiritual teacher)
Strengths	Extremely sensitive, deep, wise, quirky, devoted, mystical, emotional, a teacher and guide, pool of reflection for us
Emotional default	Fear
Season	Winter
Organs	Kidney/bladder
Time	3:00 p.m. – 7:00 p.m.
Sense organ	Ears
Sense	Hearing
Coat color	Often all black, or black/white or black/brown
Common issues	Bone and joint issues, bladder, kidney, fertility, thyroid
Wants	Connection, trust, peace, evolution of their human in all ways
Needs	Quiet and peace, safety, deep connection with their human
Stressors	Emotional insensitivity and dishonesty, chaos, loud noises, energetic influences like pesticides, chemical shampoos or cleaners, and power lines
Response to stress	Strange behavior, odd physical ailments, panic
Stress balancers	Maintaining a deep and intimate connection with their human, emotional honesty, rest, elimination of energetic disruptions
Supportive therapies	Energy healing such as Reiki, acupressure, help from animal communicators, herbal/homeopathic/Bach flower remedies
Relationship support	Trust and accept her as your teacher and guide

ability to shapeshift from vapor to mist to rain, to ice, snow, and sleet—and so does your Water Dog. Each one of the five elements can suddenly appear in her personality and along with it, the element's behaviors. So, know that when you see your dog shifting and changing, it's just your Water Dog wearing one of her other elemental "masks."

In time you may be able to see what triggers this masking. In my experience, age can have a lot to do with it. Water element puppies try out all the elements on a regular basis until they figure out what best suits their home life. In addition, seasons can prompt a different element to show up for that specific time of year and Water Dogs will flow strongly with each seasonal change. Also, certain circumstances, both long-term and short-term, can prompt a Water Dog to imitate a particular element for safety, all the while carrying the deeply ingrained fear they feel underneath—their default emotion. And lastly, Water takes the shape of whatever contains it, so be honest and true to who you are.

Water Dogs are emotional beings and also extremely sensitive to our human emotions. They are pools of reflection for us. Do not expect to get away with acting differently than you actually feel around them; the Water Dog will know. They are the quintessential empaths. Accept this gift of reflection and utilize it to create a deeper connection with them and hopefully with your own self. On a higher level, your personal growth is their ultimate goal. If you truly listen, Water Dogs will remind you of both their deep ancestral wisdom and your own.

Water Dogs learn best when they have a deep and intimate connection with their human. They are extremely smart and devoted. Their emotional reflex is fear, often deep, visceral fear. Just like water, they can be calm one moment and go into a full-blown overflowing torrent of panic the next. Water Dogs are sadly often passed around from owner to owner for odd behaviors that are not seemingly manageable or understandable to most humans. But they truly are amazing, loving, cuddly, and fun partners when you are ready for them. Stay the course with your Water Dog, they are worth it! And they definitely have many things to teach you if you truly listen.

Water elements, both animal and human, often come into this life with a traumatic beginning. It makes total sense that the karmic issues they are working through have to do with fear, trust, sharing their empathic wisdom, and being the authentic being that they truly are, no masks, no running, no hiding. In this life journey, Water elements can learn to manage fear by being still and honoring the situation instead of running like a frightened deer. This is a life-changing process. By accessing their ability for deep stillness, they access their own true power. They learn to trust others, trust themselves, and feel safe to be who they truly are as they gently reflect others' emotions. Water elements can hear the voices of our ancestors who are asking all of us to honor and hone our vital sensitivities.

The Story of Pretzel

Pretzel, my now fourteen-month-old Water element dog, has gone through each element more times in her first year of life than I can count. Some days it is several in a day! She is predominantly Water (seen by her reactions to stress). She is secondly a Wood Dog—learning her athletic ability, pushing and testing boundaries. And as I am writing this, we are entering early summer—Fire element season—so she is displaying really kooky, fun behavior and also needs lots of deep, cuddly moments.

Pretzel was a feral rescue pup, now young adult, who was born under a drug house with a starved no-milk mother, dying and dead siblings, and crazy chaos from the human world above and around her. I was told she resisted capture and I believe she had a very traumatic experience during that capture (as if her early puppy life wasn't traumatic enough). At the time I was looking for a puppy partner for Wilbur, and Pretzel showed up in an online search. She looked exactly like the puppy photos of my last beloved Water Dog, Luna, who had passed away two years prior. The photos were uncanny—the same black puppy with white chest blaze shaped like a flying goose, speckled paws and white dots on the back of her hind feet, the same piercing amber eyes, the same mix-breed puppy body, and that same intense, precocious, intelligent look in her eyes that Luna wore as a young pup. I actually pulled out my Luna puppy photos just to compare and could have sworn they were the same dog. I scooped her up as quickly as possible and then was told her sad early puppyhood history, similar to Luna who was dropped in a shelter night box as a puppy with her starved siblings.

When we first met Pretzel, it took my husband Mark and me over an hour to be able to touch her, her fear of humans was so deep and visceral. There was no aggression, only fast, fearful avoidance techniques that were sharply honed. Mark and I have dedicated our lives to helping and healing animals, and between the two of us we have worked with thousands of animals in pain or distress. Our work has included street dogs internationally, urban captures of mistreated animals, disaster response, wildlife humane capture situations, and of course living with our working partners—dogs. The animals have been our teachers. Our heart reflexes are open, strong, patient, and wise, and the animals feel that. Our listening skills are "ways of being" with animals, that gently affect our ways of doing. When we listen with our open hearts, this creates a vibrational coherence that honors the animal's personal safety zone and makes them feel more comfortable with us.

Pretzel eventually felt this and allowed us in, but only for a tender moment where we saw her sweet potential and hesitant willingness. The door quickly shut but already our hearts had fallen in love with this tiny adorable, wounded Water being.

Pretzel is still highly sensitive and after nine months of intermittent exposure to others, she still is extremely fearful of humans, except the small core people in her life—myself, my husband, our loving dog sitter Cheryle, and sometimes one or two neighbors. In her own environment and on our trail walks she is timidly curious about other humans. But if on leash and walking about town, she is terrified when a person walks towards us head on, or puts a hand out towards her. The fear is, and may always be, a visceral reflex for her, programmed deeply from her traumatic formative early months as that hungry, feral puppy.

At home, Pretzel is an entirely different being. Confident and precocious, full of herself, bossing Wilbur around during play, showing off her intelligence, she is fun and lovable. She loves touch and often demands it. She's also incredibly verbal, even musical. Daily she includes herself in our human discussions, mirroring and intoning both our voices. She asks for anything she wants or needs—food, potty, or play—with high pitched squeaks, burbles, yips, long and loud yawns, and play growls. She also asks me at 8:50 p.m. every night to play my flute so she can sing. And sing she does! She tries to match all the notes, keys, and stair steps I make with my flute. After that she sleeps soundly through the night. The Water element sense is hearing and she has translated that into her own musical and verbal prowess. She is one of the most overtly communicative and hilarious dogs I've ever had.

At this early age I see Pretzel activating the natural intense stillness of the Water element when she is "hunting" bunnies or robins. She rarely catches one but finds her fun spending an incredibly long time—up to 30 minutes—in one position watching them. Or she stalks them, moving her limbs Qi gong-like with intensive slowness—one leg in five minutes, the next leg in five minutes. It is transfixing and fascinating to watch. I am sure her rough feral beginnings partly shaped both this movement potential and her natural elemental affinity for deep, focused stillness.

As a handler and healer of many dogs, I maintain myself as a strong, kind, confident leader with a listening heart and an observant and caring nature. I take her everywhere with me but also honor her ever-shifting tolerance levels for even mild social stimulus. I always watch, support, and praise for the little improvements we make along the way. There is an old adage I learned years ago and now embrace deeply: the most important social relationship an animal can have is with their own human.

It takes courage, time, and a good understanding partner. Water without a vessel to hold it cannot truly understand or heal its karmic lessons. Each day Pretzel becomes a little bit more of her true self. Each day, I become a better partner.

Best Practices for Working
with Water Dogs

Pretzel is one of many Water element animals that have come into my life. There were Luna, Cedar, Grizzly, several Water element horses, a few cats, and many clients' animals, usually serial rescues or feral animals. All of them have graced my life with the mystery and magic that comes with their acute sensitivity and higher purpose. It seems they often come into this life with trauma, thus developing deep sensitivities. They are here to serve a purpose for whoever can find the patience and openness to understand and work with their quirkiness. It is often a life-changing experience on many levels for the person who lives with a Water element animal.

I've seen many clients and people give up on their Water animals and rehome them. Some animals move from person to person because of the challenging behaviors they've developed due to human misunderstanding and their own fears. I have never judged people for that; the timing for accepting teachings is different for everyone. The Water element animal may have ended up with the wrong person and often gets rehomed to the perfect person.

I've also seen many people find the richness, connection, and wondrous teachings that come from life with the Water element animal. Once they understand this element, it is a magical ride down a river of fascination, evolution, and spiritual growth for both human and animal. These patient, caring humans often describe feeling blessed to have Water animals in their life.

As like attracts like, I too am a Water element, as are many of the humans who embrace Water animals. As rivers run to the ocean, so Water finds Water—when the timing is right for both.

To help Water Dogs make their way through life, they need a strong, kind, devoted leader that does not rattle easily. They need to have a strong trust bond with their human. Once they bond with you, they will often look to you first, before letting their own fear lead them. This energetically interactive relationship is important to Water Dogs. Their strong empathic ability will read your solidness (or lack of it), and rapidly pattern behaviors and reactions from that. There is a feralness in all Water element beings. Learn to nurture and honor that latent wildness and the transparent connection between you and your Water Dog. You will catch their fears before they turn into complete chaos.

Common Ailments in Water Dogs

Water Dogs often have mysterious ailments and injuries that come and go, or may not be easily diagnosed by or respond to conventional medicine. Kidney and bladder are their yin and yang organs respectively. They can be prone to kidney issues, bladder infections, and weak lower backs and hind ends. Water Dogs and humans often have a long back which can cause spinal instability. The bladder meridian runs along the spine, carrying energy to many nerve roots that exit the spine and supply the organs. When imbalanced, this can cause a cascade of problems. Keeping them strong in both their core and body can help with that. Visit your vet for blood and urine tests at least once a year as they age. Water Dogs will always teach you to think out of the box, and are strongly asking you to trust your intuition about making decisions that feel right for them.

Water Dogs are like a canary in a coal mine. They are very sensitive to external energetic influences such as toxic chemicals, herbicide spraying, pesticides, EMFs (electromagnetic frequencies) and power lines. These can bring on some of the mystery ailments that baffle us. Respect that you have an extremely sensitive being and honor their wisdom while also considering these effects on yourself and others in your household.

My favorite saying after living and working with many Water element dogs is "expect the unexpected." You will see, hear, and witness some very interesting, deliberate, and bizarre behaviors steeped in deep wisdom, humor, and very clear intention. Learn from the Water Dog's wisdom and they will enrich your life with their purpose and presence for years to come.

Water Dog Life Lesson
Do not give up on your Water Dog but look within yourself. If you listen deeply you will find there is a river of teaching she is guiding you through. You may not see it right away but it will show itself when the time is right.

Water Element Rescue Dogs – Searching for the Spirit Dog

The Water Dog is another misunderstood creature that is rehomed far too often. These dogs can mask all the elements and so can have all the quirks and positive aspects of the other four elements while also wearing the mysterious quirks and essence of the Water Dog. These are the dogs that are looking terribly fearful in the back of the kennel while simultaneously staring you straight in the eyes with a petrified look. They may curiously slink forward and stop, almost flat, then slink forward again, always keeping eye contact, while still being hypervigilant about their surroundings at the same time. They are sizing you up as they move towards you, wanting to feel loved, wanting to be saved, wanting to find their forever, understanding partner.

The Water Dog's sense is hearing. Every little noise elicits a response, particularly in a heightened state of fear. Fear is their emotional reflex—not just fear, but visceral deep-rooted fear that can prompt fast physical retreats. Being misunderstood and fearful, these animals have seen a lot in life, usually from the time their eyes open. They also carry past karma that may have predated the inherent Water elemental fear itself. They connect extremely deeply when they find the right person. That person needs to be patient and have a solid mind and clear heart.

If you find yourself drawn to that sad slinking dog in the kennel and want to save them for a reason you can't explain, you should probably consider taking them home. The pull towards these animals is deeper than the conscious mind, but it requires a strong commitment. And not just a commitment to the Water Dog, but a commitment to yourself to learn all you can from this amazing, mystical being. These animals will reflect teachings and contracts that you are supposed to enter into in this lifetime. As you learn about yourself and your Water element dog, a swift current will carry you downstream to a new way of being in the world.

Although these dogs are our soulful teachers, they are often hilariously funny, extremely intelligent, and great adventure partners. They truly "go with the flow." They will take you on a journey to create a deep bond and connection between you, them, and the wildness within you. They need a solid partner that is not afraid of this, or afraid of life. Water Dogs ask for that support in exchange for what they bring to us. They are like truth serum, showing you your truth as you walk in this world.

Adopting a Water Dog may sound daunting and a little scary, but when you are ready for them and you feel that tug, you are ready for their gifts. Learning, laughter, love, deep connection flows into your life and cleanses your spirit, heart, and mind. What better gift is there?

Water Dog Quiz
1 = Never true	2 = Sometimes true	3 = Always true
I am not very sociable with other dogs or humans
I tend to retreat within myself for safety and rest
I am wary of humans and their motives
I am very curious about bugs, smells, people's skin, toes, socks, birds, new household items
I often hide behind my handler when in groups
I love learning new things
I have a complex inner and lively self that I only show to my close handler or partner
I am happy to follow and not lead
I am playful when I feel loved
I want someone to love and understand me

	I can be persistent
	I am easygoing with changes in routine
	I can fall into visceral fear easily or be completely fearless, to my disadvantage
	It takes me time to trust someone
	My movement flows like water
	I speak a lot and am a good clear communicator in other ways
	I can be suspicious of humans
	I never forget past hurts and pains
	I can easily change elements to suit the circumstance
	Home is my safe haven
	Water Element Dog Total

The Old Water Dog

Old Water Dogs hold a wellspring of wisdom in their beings. We often see this in their deep, soulful eyes. They have "been there, done that" on so many otherworldly levels, as well as this one we now live in.

Old Water Dogs need to feel quiet, peaceful, yet still connected with you as they age. Knowing they always have your deep connection and devotion allows them to access their own inner stillness, which is a normal part of aging. Old Water Dogs will still hold a powerful endurance and soft inner strength, even when it seems they do not. Water is a source of life for sharing and creates growth and resilience. These Water animals carry this resilience in their DNA, sourced from their wise ancestral roots. They understand reciprocity and bond deeply to those they support and who support them. They show their gratitude by being their kooky but authentic selves and can still shapeshift elements at any given moment. And they may often drop into your dreams to chat; don't be afraid to listen!

Old Water Dogs prefer to be right by your side if they can be. Keep their muscles and back strong with movement. The Water element rules the spine, bones, and nervous system as well as the lymphatic system, so it is important to support these vital systems as well as their yin/yang organs, kidney and bladder. Doing the Good Morning Spinal Wakeup (see page 38) daily can help the old ones feel less stiff and put a bounce in their step!

Water Dogs often do best with energy healing techniques such as acupressure, reiki, EFT, and animal communication. They always have a lot to say and animal communicators love talking to a Water animal. Start ramp training early in their life as they tend to weakness in the hind end and may have problems jumping into cars and climbing steps. Slings can be very helpful also. Watch for excess drinking and urination, and be sure to schedule a vet visit if you see this.

The Old Water Dog has hopefully had a profound influence on your life and needs to know you have moved along on your own inner journeys. Be open to their communications in both this life and your dreamtime. Their spirit will always be watching you!

Old Water Dog Life Lesson
Don't let fear take you off course in your soul's journey. Believe, follow your nose and your heart, and just like water, you will travel beyond your limits and support the world around you.

Issues for Older Water Dogs

Stressors: Chaos, lack of trust, loud noises, emotional dishonesty, weak hind end, bladder, adrenal and kidney issues.

Response to Stress: Deeply embedded fear, lack of connection and appetite, frequent urination.

Stress Balancers: Deep connection with person/handler, honesty, trust, emotional, physical, and spiritual closeness, energy healing and herbs, lack of chaos.

Relationship Support: Old Water Dogs need to consistently feel the same love, trust, and devotion they gave you during your journey with them.

Acupressure Points
for the Water Dog

Please refer to the guidelines for acupressure in Chapter 2, page 34.

CAUTION: Do not use these points on pregnant animals!

Bladder 60 (BL 60) "Kunlun Mountain" is a full body aspirin point. It relieves back pain and neck stiffness. It also strengthens the back and weak hind ends. It is located in the deep hollow on the outside of the dog's hind leg hock joint. See image below (Figure 11).

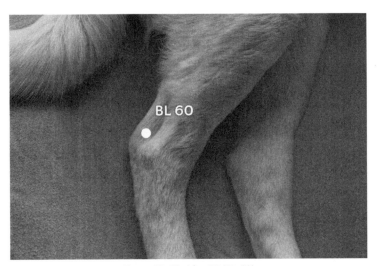

Figure 11: Bladder 60 (BL 60)

NOTE: BL 60 is a powerful combination with LI 4 (Wood) for dogs in acute or chronic pain. For chronic pain these points can be done daily.

Kidney 3 (KI 3) "Great Stream" strengthens the lumbar spine, is good for arthritis of the hock joint, and helps restore the immune system. It is located on the inside of the dog's hind leg hock joint directly across from BL 60. See image below (Figure 12).

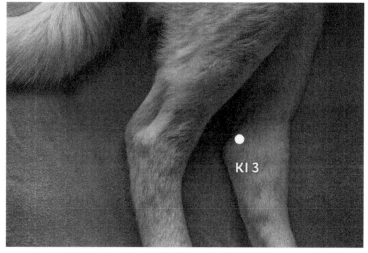

Figure 12: Kidney 3 (KI 3)

You can treat both points BL 60 and KI 3 at the same time by gently "pinching" your fingers around the hock. This creates a synergistic effect in the body.

PART 3

The Relationship with the Humans

8. Now, Who Are You?

At times you have to leave the city of your comfort and go into the wilderness of your intuition. What you'll discover will be wonderful. What you'll discover is yourself.

—ALAN ALDA

As you start to view your dog's world in this new way, consider broadening your scope onto yourself and envision which element might fit you. Try each element on for size. What actual element in nature do you resonate with? Where in nature do you go to recharge? What element makes you feel good or comfortable? Or uncomfortable? Answering these questions—with your feelings overriding your thoughts—can provide a unique and helpful understanding of your own inner and outer world. The ultimate goal is learning the warp, weave, and blending of your relationship with your dog while also shining light on your relationships with others and the world around you.

First of all, remember that like your dog, you inhabit all of the elements. And as the seasons change, our elements change. This applies also to the seasons of life; as we age we move into other seasonal elements, often ending our journey in the winter season of life—the wise and mysterious Water element that can grace us with easy travel into the next realm.

Human elements, and humans in general, are much more complex in their life experiences, interactions, and relationships than dogs. If we are both lucky, our dogs live on average one-seventh of our lifetime. This means a dog's experiences, interactions, and relationships are not only less complex than ours, but also shorter-lived. It may be much easier initially to discover a dog's element than a human's element.

We humans, due to our complex lives and distractions, are not as close to the rhythms of nature as our dogs are. A human's life experiences can create long-lasting effects on our psyche, minds, and hearts and shadow our connections to both nature and our true selves. All this can complicate our personalities and our responses to life and stress. In general, animals resonate better with their genetic connection to nature than most humans. An animal's body is meant to sniff and search the air, to see far and wide, and to sense the earth with their paws on the ground. Their deeper connection to nature shows us a truer, undiluted version of each element in each dog.

With time and some honest clarity, you will discover one or two predominant elements that reflect your own human traits, foibles, default emotions, needs, wants, and ways of being and doing. Start with what clearly stresses you and be aware of how you react to it and deal with it. This shouldn't be hard as stress happens to most of us on a daily basis. When stressed I always say, "In my next life, I want to be one of my dogs!"

Knowing your primary archetypal element greatly increases your self-awareness. Your archetype helps you discover all that you bring to the world in your own unique way. It also shows you your deep-rooted, unconscious reactions to stress and helps you learn to cope with life's challenges. Knowing your primary archetypal element will also help you predict and avoid difficult reactions and unsettling behavior patterns. Such awareness goes a long way towards managing coping skills and creating a better relationship with yourself and everyone around you, including your dog.

You may initially find it easier to quietly investigate other humans with this new lens. Often it is easier to gain a bird's-eye view on someone else as opposed to ourselves. Just be graceful and very careful about making any suggestions to the human object of your investigation. You may want to keep your discoveries to yourself until you establish a really clear vision of each element and a really clear vision about who you are and how you both interact.

Here is a good way to start your own elemental journey and gain safe feedback on who you are. If you have a friend or partner who knows you well, briefly share the characteristics of each Five Element dog and human story with them; have your quick reference pages and quizzes bookmarked for you both to refer to. Then be brave, take a big breath, and ask them to be gentle but honest in their feedback to help you dive into discovering your own archetypal element. A good friend will see you for who you are and bring an honest, loving clarity to the table. They will also be curious about themselves. This can create an even deeper understanding and friendship between the two of you.

Figuring out personal elements can also be fun table talk for families and long-time friends. It may lend some needed understanding and harmony to your lives together. Understanding has a way of softening our judgments and the barriers we create. It can help harmonize our relationships with others and of course, with ourselves.

Try to see the echo of the dog elements in your own human elements. We all, four-legged and two-legged, ultimately walk with the same spirit of elemental personalities, behaviors, needs, wants, and stressors, whether in boots, paws, heels, or hooves. And as with everything in this complex world of humans, there are multitudes of Five Element recipes for personalities. There are several great books specifically on human Five Element personality in the resource section of this book if you care to dive deeper. I would strongly encourage reading them.

This book started with understanding our dogs better and harmonizing our relationships with them. Our dogs are truly our teachers in life. They will always guide us and challenge us to make the world a better, kinder place. Now that we have learned about the Five Element personalities of our dogs, we can look at ourselves and other human beings through the Five Element lens. The understanding we previously gained will echo out into all our relationships, from the simplest ones, such as the grumpy grocery store clerk, to the deepest and most precious ones, such as our partners, friends, and family.

Brief Overview of the Human Elements

WOOD: "Army Sergeant"

Likes to be in charge and will take charge if no one else does. Athletic, competitive in all ways, solid under pressure, has strong determination and endurance, fast learner, strong finisher. Anger is default emotion along with frustration, impatience, and any offshoots of anger. Strong, purposeful and powerful, especially in springtime.

FIRE: "Diva"

Life of the party, a bright light for others, has charismatic magnetism (people suddenly ignore others just to be near a Fire element), needs a strong social life. Joy and fun are very important, wants others to be happy, is a fun and easy friend. Overly joyful bordering on kooky at times, easily ungrounded, drama queen when stressed. Needs to know they are loved, often is a great salesperson and might dabble as a politician, inspiring teacher, or healer. Default emotion is excess joy which can lead to a disturbance of the Shen or panic attacks. Loves summer but can't tolerate too much heat.

EARTH: "Caregiver"

Kind, gentle, nurturer, caregiver, can't say no to helping someone. Soft or no boundaries, foodie, possible weight management issues, solid, dependable and unflappable but worries a lot and can be stubborn or obsessive. Does best with regular rhythms, particularly with food, loves naps, gives great hugs. Default emotion is worry. Loves late summer and early autumn.

METAL: "Librarian"

Gobbles up knowledge and facts and loves to share them, detailed, charges forward with purpose in life. May be rigid in body, belief structures, and relationships, can be critical and judgmental. Given time, can be your most loyal friend. Default emotion is grief. Most comfortable in late autumn and early winter.

WATER: "Empathic One"

Highly sensitive, mystical, empathic, creative, emotional, deep feeler and thinker. Goes with the flow, reflects and feels emotions/actions of others, bonds deeply. A supportive guide for others' growth, carries ancestral wisdom, powerful enduring nature, often misunderstood, humble, seeks stillness. Default emotion is fear. Winter is safe season to go deep within.

The Human Scenario

A team of five humans, all with different primary elements, are working on a project together . . .

- The Water excitedly dreams up, designs, and presents the project idea, names it, and creates the tag lines and sales handles before the project ever gets started.

- The Wood rallies the team together, oversees the process, assigns each person to their task, presents a detailed work list, removes any obstacles, and sees the project to the finish line.

- The Fire cheers everyone on, fills in as needed, keeps things light and lively, has fun with their tasks, praises everyone else, quickly suggests solutions when the project flags, and lifts spirits when the rest of the team is down. Oh, and they gently insist with a smile that everyone goes out for a beer together on Fridays. They may even try to start a regular pickleball game!

- The Earth supports the project and the team in any way they can while sharing their own talents with confidence and humble pride, gives team hugs to everyone when unseen complications are vanquished, and verbalizes their genuine pride for others' accomplishments. They listen with a gentle ear and heart, always ready for anyone's woes, tiredness, or complaints, often bring in snacks and baked goods, and spread love and support to everyone.

- The Metal thoroughly analyzes, handles, and double-checks all the fine details and if needed refines any processes that need fixing, constructively debating ideas and changes.

They show up for work on time and work late if needed. They might be inflexible in dealing with others' wants, and tolerate or hide from any hugs or social events.

When the elements all work together toward a common goal they can create a balanced circle of cooperation. We see it here in this scenario. Each element has its own gifts, timing, and actions that they bring to the table. This creates a cooperative working system just as in nature, each contributing something to the whole. We can see this in successful business teams, athletic teams, and many other common activities and creations in life.

Community needs diversity, nature teaches us that. Diversity of mind, body, spirit, and ideas is the glue that holds our world together. It creates a foundation and scaffolding for many visions, visions that change our lives. Find your element gifts and share them, be equitable, be humble, listen to others and fill in the gaps. We are all in this together!!

Amazing Humans
Living Their Elements

You will see from some of the following stories that the elemental concepts are the same for dogs and humans, but the life applications are different. These are all real-life people, living true to their archetypal elements while contributing to the whole.

Also notice how secondary and tertiary elements can soften or complement their primary elements. This can create a more balanced human experience. Finding your secondary and tertiary elements, and even your hibernating fourth and fifth elements, can help you see the whole vision of yourself and give you confidence in your uniqueness. You'll discover your special talents—no need to push a square peg in a round hole!

Gauge your element percentages from the quizzes located after each element story. What truly is your genuine competition level? Is Wood your element number one or number three? If you are a number one or two Fire, gravitate more towards your social life. Or number one Metal—not social! Learn more, and do good things for the world. Maybe you are number one Metal but a number two Fire—great combination for networking and purposeful business success or teaching! Fire, create that non-profit you have been dreaming of. If you have a strong Earth, increase your love and nurturing and spend more time with family. Primary Waters — become the visionary you are and find those who can help make your vision a reality and see it to the finish line.

As you learn how to live from this elemental perspective, the world will open up for you and things that aren't working will be replaced with the things you are supposed to be doing in life. Your focus in life will be clearer and more cohesive. Your relationships will thrive and so will you!

Wood Element

My husband, Mark, is a Wood element with a second and third element of Water and Earth, respectively. Mark is a natural and kind leader. He easily steps into the role of leader if needed—and sometimes even if it is not needed, which is often appreciated by others. He has always been strong and athletic and still is at age 67. His nature can be competitive in a quiet, fair way, having learned that from his amazing parents and brothers, and from his black belt in Aikido. As a wildlife veterinarian who has worked with grizzly bears, mountain lions, wolves, most North American wildlife as well as street dogs and disaster rescue around the world, he is very solid under pressure. Mark is a natural leader of teams (Wood), a sought-after teacher in his field (Wood), well respected by his students and colleagues (Wood), needs quiet rest time to contemplate, debrief, and reboot himself after giving his all (Water), and is always available to lend a hand (Earth).

When Mark's Wood is imbalanced his competitiveness creates impatience, defensiveness, grumpiness, and occasional apathy that quickly turns into an overactive mental state. This causes him to wake up between 1:00 and 3:00 a.m. at night—Liver/Wood time. A balanced Wood element innately reflexes to anger but does not always react (action). They can manage and channel the energy of anger if they have good self-awareness—balance is the key. Mark is this way. I often see him working through things when he is angry and gaining more strength instead of giving in to roaring.

During imbalanced times his Water element also precipitates some fear that he doesn't quite understand. His Earth worries and he gets a wee bit stubborn. These issues are rare, but easy to see and catch when they pop up because he is such a solid, balanced Wood ninety-nine percent of the time.

When Mark is imbalanced, I try to expand his intense inner focus outwardly back to the world around him, as is needed for Wood elements. I suggest a bike ride or something to get him moving, just as I would do with a Wood Dog. A walk in the quiet forest also helps him reboot his Wood element. Time on the beach or in the kayak, where he can scan the expansive water for whales or bald eagles, is helpful to bring some nurturing Water back in and have his strong Wood sight mechanisms stimulated. He can also create an energetic shift with garden chores, or time on the stair stepper, though his Earth imbalance fights it sometimes, wanting to be a lump on the couch. But once he gets moving he comes home to his strong, reliable, determined Wood self again.

When Wood becomes imbalanced it can tip the scales on the other supportive elements. If Mark wears himself out working long hours on the computer or teaching, his Wood element becomes overburdened and imbalanced. Because he has a secondary Water element, it is a natural reflex to revert to this element to nourish his Wood. Water feeds Wood. The Water element can transform the imbalances of Wood by feeding it quiet rest and deep introspective time while regulating the flow of tasks and energy. Wood elements often need the inherent peace and harmony of Water to help feed and rebalance wood, just as in nature. A Wood having Water as a second element can help the Wood ease back into balance without much effort.

Mark is also an amazing caregiver who often puts others first, is incredibly supportive, and loves to cook and eat yummy food. He does well with routine, showing his tertiary Earth element. He occasionally will show an imbalance in his Earth element by worrying or obsessing. The Earth element supports the deep rootedness of the Wood element and helps it stabilize but earth indulgences can be overly supportive, bringing on imbalance. It's common for a number three Earth to step in to support a number one Wood with self-care and snacks. Think of a tall deep-rooted tree that needs the earth to support and balance it, allowing expansion for the many roots that grow throughout its years. These trees support and house many other beings and need the support of other elements such as Earth and Water to thrive. Overall this is a good balance to find in a strong Wood element person.

Mark is currently in the life cycle season of the Metal element. I watch him recognizing, refining, and recreating his purposefulness in both life and work. He is gobbling up new languages (librarian Metal and fast learner Wood) related to online work, computer programs, and woodworking techniques, to name a few. I see his vulnerable sensitivities (Metal) when he allows them to surface, and his need for quiet and focused recovery (Metal) after a long day. Mark's life cycle Metal element plays a powerful role as Metal controls Wood in the control (Ko) cycle. At this stage of Mark's life cycle, Metal is the final element to clean up and repurpose his Wood element when he is imbalanced or off-kilter.

As the spring Wood season approaches, I can see how vibrantly balanced or subtly imbalanced Mark is. Is he bursting forth with new ideas or overly competitive, obsessive, grumpy, irritated, or restless?

Wood Element Human Quiz
1 = Never true | 2 = Sometimes true | 3 = Always true
I am courageous and determined in life
I don't change my mind easily once I make a decision
I am honest and dependable
I love to compete
I have intense focus
I like to be in charge or a leader and will naturally fill that void if there is one

	I can reflex to anger, impatience, frustration
	I have strong personal boundaries
	I do not like having my time wasted by someone
	I perform well and sometimes my best, under stress
	I am a very good and effective communicator
	I am a hard worker and expect the same from others
	I can be critical or judgmental
	It's hard for me to delegate
	I have a hard time relaxing
	I can be compassionate and very generous when there is a need
	I can lose my temper easily
	I love challenges and thrive to succeed in life
	I love to exercise and do challenging sports
	I want control over all things in my life
	Wood Element Total

Fire Element

I have known so many beautiful, tender, and gregarious Fire people in my lifetime. They are the vibrant, socially active people who are always spreading goodness, gratitude, and light everywhere they go. They look straight into your eyes with their heart and smile a smile that makes you smile back. Fires have a way of lifting your mood like a playful balloon.

They crave fun and excitement and are quick-minded and quick-witted, always ready with a gentle joke to make someone smile. They are true masters at joy and lighthearted connection. Fires will generously listen to others, often answering with praise or an uplifting comment. Fire elements carry the light of the sun in their pockets and share it with grace, ease, and sincerity. Their inner warmth and outer charisma make them magnets for other humans. We are drawn to them like a moth to the flame.

Fires tend to cruise through life wearing the proverbial rose-colored glasses, the eternal optimists. When Fire elements imbalance or allow themselves to endure stress, they crash and burn hard. They often panic and become unglued. They will rely on others to ground them, calm them, and tickle the joy back inside them so they can recover. Fire humans can live with chronic anxiety. Fires also have a strong emotional awareness that allows them to recognize their own emotional state. This awareness prompts them to reach out to others for support. With help from friends they can quickly climb the ladder back up to the sun and go on their merry way spreading more fiery goodness.

Cedar is a young man I know, the son and grandson of my dear friends Sarah and Joy, respectively. He is very much a Fire, with fiery red hair, an easy way about him, and always a smile and a good word. I often have an inner giggle that his name is Cedar—a famous and useful tree world-wide—and he is a Fire element; his name creating an energetic tree spirit feed that supports his primary element Fire. Sharp as a tack, he moves and talks quickly in a very upbeat, loving, and kind way. He cares deeply about his family, his mom being a Fire/Earth. I love watching the two Fires together in dialogue; they are seamless within their lightning speed discussions and smiles, finishing each other's sentences, and making my head spin as I try to keep up. Like two sparks meeting to create a flame.

Cedar has many friends, and he's gregarious and polite to others, often ending a conversation with light-hearted laughter. He occasion-ally spins off around the world for adventures, sometimes helping with environmental causes. Cedar is all heart and empathy as he talks gently to his ninety-three-year-old grandmother, Joy (another perfect Fire element person and name!), a matriarch in a long line of Fire elements.

It warms my heart to see this young vibrant spirit living true to his element. It is inspiring to me and to our future to see a young man so upbeat and concerned about others. Like a warm fire on a cold night, Cedar will grace those around him with comfort and smiles, as is the family tradition.

Fire Element Human Quiz	
1 = Never true | 2 = Sometimes true | 3 = Always true	
	I love stimulating environments
	I often feel joy and try to spread it around to others
	I love being the life of the party
	I like people and love being around others
	I love to dance and laugh and have fun
	I feel others' emotions and try to help cheer them up when they need it
	I love telling stories and tend to exaggerate a bit just for fun
	I am an optimist at heart even when things aren't going well
	I can panic easily
	I can lapse into periods of anxiety
	My heart can range from broken to exhilarated in moments
	I like to move and am not good at sitting very long
	I love high energy exercise classes
	I love meeting new people
	People tell me I smile through my words
	I love making people smile
	I can easily get scatterbrained and disorganized
	My attention hops around and I can have trouble staying focused
	I have a hard time saying no
	I can exhaust myself from too much fun
	Fire Element Total

Earth Element

I am lucky to have a beautifully balanced Earth element as one of my closest friends. Terry is the most nurturing, kind, grounded, and refreshing human I know. She is the one person in my life that I go to for the very best "squishy" hugs full of love and tenderness, always perfectly timed for when I need them. She is an awesome mother, an incredibly dependable friend, and a resilient caregiver for her aging mother, her family and friends, and her animals—always there when you need her, family first, and completely devoted to those she loves.

Several years ago, I sustained a serious injury. With husband Mark out of town teaching, my Earth element friend patiently and lovingly tended to me in the most natural and beautiful way—I felt like I was being cared for by Mother Teresa herself. It was a powerful panacea for my broken body and troubled spirit. Earth element humans and dogs can innately heal with their love and gestures and will generously give to those in need, especially those lucky ones closest to them. They will look deep into your eyes and heart and send the most caring energy directly into your soul. Although deep inside they need and enjoy praise and gratitude, they share their love freely as their nurturing comes from the purest place in their heart. It is their nature to nurture.

Earth elements also have an inner strength that is purposeful, sensitive, and fiercely protective of their flock. With that fortitude can come a strong sense of worry, mostly worn internally. My friend Terry may worry but she never lets that stop her resilient determination to help someone in need. Earth elements have long memories and tender hearts. As friends and family members, we should respect their gentleness and kindness and always offer our best version of our truest self to them.

We all have more than one element and Terry has a secondary Metal element that she wears very well. She is highly intelligent, very experienced and detailed in life and business, while passionate about purposeful projects. Her Metal element weaves in well with her strong Earth. In the Five Element Sheng (creation) cycle, Earth births Metal so they fit together easily. The Metal element imbalance that causes rigidity rarely shows up on my balanced Earth/Metal friend although she grieves (Metal) long and deeply for the loss of loved ones. When her Metal imbalances, it is quickly rebalanced by her expansive and protective Earth tenderness. Severe Metal element imbalances are often centered in a place of fierce self-protection and armor and can result in cutting or burying any ties with someone who has wronged them. My Earth friend Terry carries the promise of all the good tenets of the Metal element and that makes for a happy Earth/Metal mix!

Terry's third element is a quiet Water. She is quite fey and very tuned in with the natural world. She sees and hears things most people miss and basks in the wonders of our Earth and nature. She is highly empathic, feels what others feel, especially animals, and enjoys communing with her resident owl families. Her soft Water element communicates with those beings who have passed on that she loves, in simple ways that only she notices. She is a gift, she is Earth!

Earth Element Human Quiz
1 = Never true | 2 = Sometimes true | 3 = Always true
I love spending time with my family
I love having children and animals around me
I love supporting others
I am always available for my friends when they need me
I feel deep compassion and empathy for others
I will go out of my way to help others
I am very loyal
I don't like change
I worry a lot
I sometimes obsessively worry
I sometimes get obsessive with food
I love to hug and people love my hugs

	I love to nurture
	I want my home and personality to be comfortable for everyone
	I like non-competitive group exercise
	I don't easily share my problems with others
	I can be stubborn
	I can be overprotective
	I can gain weight easily
	I love sugar and carbohydrates
	Earth Element Human Total

Metal Element

Our friend Joe is an amazing woodworker and teacher. He is a kind, caring, and gentle Metal element living a purposeful life. Like many Metals, he is also strong willed and determined. Joe deeply understands wood and has the ability to repurpose, shape, define, and enhance the core essence of any piece of wood that comes his way. Who better to have these gifts than a Metal element! In the Ko (control) cycle, Metal chops or controls Wood and can magically shape it into a beautiful object for a future life beyond the mighty tree it once was.

Joe runs our local woodshop and is a natural teacher, as most Metals are. His woodworking classes help young people realize they can define their own vision, shape their own purpose, and create their own designs in life. Interestingly, these students are often in the Wood element life cycle stage of spring. Metals tend to be good guides and they can use their unique sensitivities to carefully and precisely approach even those more "troubled" youth. Hands are directly connected to mind and heart. Woodworking is the opportunity to guide them to their own irrefutable evidence that they can change and transform things. The end result of their work is in their hands: it's beautiful, valuable, and undeniable.

Joe has discovered that craftsmanship teaches confidence. Metals have a keen attention to detail and precision. Greater levels of precision in life leads to more confidence. His adult students have the benefit of a lifelong love of wood. They want to understand wood better and respectfully work with it to maintain and enhance its beauty. At the same time there is usually a particular purpose or project in mind; Joe helps them tune in and understand what the wood is saying, how it communicates with their hands, hearts, and minds, while giving them insight on how best to shape it. Joe is a living lesson on how to live a healthy, balanced life full of sensitivity, careful listening and observation, and giving back.

Joe is now seated in his more mature Metal life cycle stage. For a primary Metal element this is a seamless transition. He freely gives his extensive knowledge, wisdom, and experience to others but also expects devotion and commitment to the task at hand. His woodworking prowess is a gift to others in many unseen ways. Like many Metals, he is an unsung hero that needs no praise or regular pats on the back, only the feeling of fulfillment of his purpose in life.

It was an "aha" moment for me when I clearly saw Joe's perfect elemental positioning in life, a Metal purposefully shaping wood to become the very best version of itself. How metaphorically perfect!

Joe also has a second element of Fire. Like Metal, Fire controls Wood. Fire also tempers Metal. Joe's Fire element shows itself in his desire to be social and interested in others' well-being and their companionship. He has a whimsical nature and a sharp-witted good humor that warms those around him, including his students. He has an ability and a desire to connect with others on purposeful projects both small and large.

Joe's wife Mary Lou is a lovely Fire/Earth combination, a perfect complement to Joe's Metal/Fire. Joe and Mary Lou's combined Fire softens and tempers his strong Metal while bringing joy to their life of purpose together. The Earth element embraces and supports Metal and births Metal's potential. Mary Lou is a biologist who also engages with students, teaching important life skills such as cooking, where she works her magic with her Earth element style. She grounds the students in lessons of the physical natural world for their own self-sufficiency. Perfect for a Fire/Earth combination!

Joe connects deeply with both humans and animals in his life. I have felt his Metal reflex of grief as his sweet Fire Dog Lilypad was aging. Joe was very soft around Lilypad and deeply concerned for her well-being and comfort. Metals can often have a shield around their hearts for protection, but Joe's balanced and caring nature along with his big-hearted Fire element dissolved this shield. Instead, I believe his memories of Lilypad still live deep within his heart. Metals can weather many storms and carry their precious memories into eternity.

With Joe's leadership skills and deep understanding of Wood and its properties, benefits, and uses, I feel strongly that his third element *is* Wood. When the elements of Metal, Fire, and Wood combine they can create strength, purpose, and life support for those around them. This is how I envision our friend Joe.

Metal Element Human Quiz
1 = Never true | 2 = Sometimes true | 3 = Always true
I am polite with others
I do not show emotion when presenting my opinions to others
I am an intellectual avidly pursuing my own interests
I try to fix what others don't notice needs fixing
My personal standards are very high
I avoid conflict
I am really not very good at having fun but prefer doing something intellectual instead
I always try to control my environment
I don't need many possessions in life
Food is secondary to work or learning
I crave solitude and quiet during my down time
I typically speak softly and with detail
I exercise with yoga, tai chi, and purposeful movement

	I need a purposeful direction in life and will create one if there isn't one
	I have very good posture
	I tend to isolate myself from humans
	I can be insensitive to others
	I over-analyze almost everything
	I am aloof and become emotionally rigid under stress
	I grieve inwardly for long periods from loss and extreme changes
	Metal Element Total

Water Element

I can intimately speak about the Water element because I am a Water element. I also have a little take-charge Wood with a wee bit of fun Fire mixed in, along with some nurturing Earth and purposeful Metal. Like most Water elements, I can mask and easily transition into any elemental form at any given moment due to circumstance, season, or whim. Water elements are the quintessential shapeshifters.

The gentle, flowing, and peaceful qualities of ponds, lakes, oceans, and rivers can be naturally present in the Water element human. And as in nature, Water humans can carry great inner strength that appears soft or hidden. When unleashed, water can turn into a tsunami, a hurricane, the carving of canyons, and the wearing down of outdated structures and vessels that have contained it. It can change temperature and reshape the world we live in. These are all examples of the power of water in our existence here on earth, omnipresent in nature, humans, and animals.

Water can also reflect what is happening in our own individual world and the world at large. Water carries deep ancestral wisdom; it is the primary source and sustenance of life. Life began and begins in water. We cannot survive without it.

Water element humans can be dynamic and deep conversationalists. And in order for them to develop trust it is vitally important that they feel heard. Waters tend to lean into their feral nature and their closeness with the natural world. They can also be playful, fun, and endlessly curious. They tend to operate on their own time schedules, preferring to stay within their own mysterious flow of magic, creativity, and imagination. When that flow is free they can be incredible artists, thinkers, and paradigm shifters. When that flow is dammed or bottled up, they lose their creative powers and may need to return to their own peaceful water-world schedule to regenerate and re-wild.

Last week was my sixty-second birthday. I chose, as I often do on my birthday, to be near water. Mark, Pretzel, and I drove a few hours to the re-wilded Elwha river located on the Olympic Peninsula in Washington State. Two separate dams were built on this river in 1947 during the rapid growth of the logging era. In 2012 and 2015, these two dams were removed and this mighty river was fully released and given back its right to flow. The transformational recovery was swift and amazing. Salmon that had been denied their ancestral spawning habitat for all those years are now part of the landscape again. The estuary, where fresh water meets salt water, has now returned to the ocean's edge and is thriving with shellfish and life. The profound rebirth of this river has benefited the entire food chain in all directions from tiny krill to orcas to humpback whales, eagles and much more. The impact of the memory of water on the natural beings who live within and around the river is profound. These memories were never lost in the many cultures of life it once supported. This river is a vital teacher for all of us about transformation and resilience.

I sat quietly by the upper river's edge, feeling and resonating with its mysterious power and its lively joy. I removed a stone I have worn around my neck for over thirty years and held it in the clear moving water. I began to feel myself soften with memories of my own restarts and new beginnings.

I've worn this stone close to my healer's heart and have ceremoniously cleaned it in many rivers, lakes, and oceans around the world. The stone looks like water, resembling the watery edges of tropical islands or river eddies, where the sky reflects on a sandy bottom at just the right depth, shining a brilliant turquoise color that is magical. It was a gift to me from a wise man of the earth who made his living finding precious stones around the world and polishing them to bring out the magical beauty and energy of each one. He said it would protect my heart as I do my healing work, that he had kept it for a long time and it was just waiting for its person. This stone has been an anchor, travel companion, and dear friend for my heart and spirit for half of my life now. Each time I sit by the water, I feel it warmly vibrate, eager to be cleaned of all it has carried and recharged with the energy of its home.

As I sat in my quietness, a mother merganser, a diving duck, caught my eye on the other side of the river. She was entering the river with her eleven, brand new merganserlings and preparing them to cross the river for what looked to be the first time. I watched as she first took them on a trial run through a small riffle of water, all eleven teeny brown bodies right behind her, bobbing like little corks as they trusted her and braved their new world. Once all eleven heads came up, Mom set off across the busy river. As I watched her and the little ones navigate and negotiate the powerful river I was struck again by the sense of new beginnings, of the innate trust that is inherent to birth and growth. The last big riffle was quite large and I held my breath as all eleven disappeared under it. After a long second, they all popped up and, seeing the close proximity of the new shore, all eleven excitedly scooted past Mom, charging to the edge and leaving her behind. My heart felt a burst of pride for their bravery and resilience. Then my heart smiled at the synchronicity of our new beginnings.

I thought of my own early beginnings, how bravely I had crossed my own wild rivers, navigating the many breaches and transformations that have occurred in my life, the changes I've weathered and adapted to. The times I've shed limitations and embraced my own power and wisdom to move into a new phase of life. Transformations that altered life as I knew it ultimately gave vibrant support to my intended journey here on Earth. I smiled while remembering how I completely bypassed any uncertainty about the changes and swam swiftly towards those new beginnings.

Many Water element humans have traumatic beginnings that shape their initial launch into the world. My life began as a Water in that typical Water element way. My birth, which my mother tearfully shared years later before she died, was filled with severe emotional trauma and drama within my parent's marital relationship. As I floated in her womb, waiting for my exit, I am certain the emotional distress my mother was enduring created a cascade of stress hormones in which I too was swimming. Due to those early circumstances and the hypervigilance I needed in my troubled family life, Water became my primary element and sanctuary. Becoming a strong Water element created the bravery, strength, resilience, and independence I needed as a child and an adult. Water still supports me with its deep wisdom, endurance, powerful inner stillness, and soft strength. It also regularly graces me with new beginnings.

Early in my equine practice, I was mentoring with a Chinese doctor and acupuncturist who spent his adult life working and teaching at a Beijing hospital before moving to the U.S. It was a busy and vibrant Wood-influenced time of my life with a booming healing business and various hard-playing seasonal sports for my fun. I would regularly visit my mentor Dr. Xiu and bring cases to discuss. I also occasionally was one of those cases and got treatments from him for various sport or horse-related injuries. He always wanted to hear my stories of how my injuries happened; it felt like he was vicariously enjoying the fun as he knew only work and family. Play had not been a big part of his life.

One day he said, "Ok, you are a Water element, right?"

"Yes, except when I'm not!"

He chuckled a full body laugh. "Don't you get scared?"

Matter-of-factly I said "No, I'm never scared."

"AHA!" he cried, "I knew it! You supposed to have fear! Fear keeps you alive!"

Dr. Xiu promptly launched into a lecture about how my Water element imbalance was caused by not having fear. I sat in surprise and awe, as visions of my fearlessness cascaded before my eyes, as well as all the injuries and potential for injuries. Something in me woke up.

Water elements are supposed to feel fear; it is their default emotion. Fear was completely foreign to me. When I did feel a tickle of it, I was able to manage it—thanks to my Wood and early life lessons—and move forward with whatever I was doing in work or play. Also, I was always around animals in pain, often large animals. I had unknowingly blocked my natural fear reflexes in order to establish trust so I could treat them when they were afraid. Animals in pain are often frightened and do not respond well to fearful people. They smell and feel our human vibrations of fear, which only reinforces their fear, especially Water element animals.

My bravery was a skill and tool that came to me naturally but now was showing its shadow side. I had all the other qualities of a Water and fit the description quite well except for this piece. After that "aha" moment for both the Doc and myself, I spent years trying to notice and feel the fear when it came, listening when it spoke to me, and pausing just a moment to consider my options. I had finally found the wisdom of fear.

Water element humans have incredible potential hiding within their mysterious ways as long as they can manage their fear, or for some, at least feel it. Waters want to run free with their ideas. Many are artists, writers, composers, philosophers, great thinkers, empathic healers, animal communicators, and creators of novel ideas and structures. They like to feel and think deeply, trying to dissect the crucial and incredible nuances of life. They are great starters of "new beginnings" but not always good finishers. They often need a village, preferably Woods and Metals, to help them get to the finish line.

Water elements can be still ponds creating quiet harmony or roaring rivers carving deep canyons with their unique ideas. Water elements can smooth over roughness in relationships while holding the balance of all life in their hands and hearts. Waters have a quiet power that transcends time and transforms lives.

Waters can also be sticky, taking on others' physical, emotional, and spiritual issues. Waters don't like or want boundaries, either in life or energetically. I have always been empathic, even long before I knew what the word meant, feeling others' feelings, whether emotional angst or physical pain. Smiles don't fool me. I often have some sudden phantom pain or jolt of emotion that is unequivocally not mine and I will look around trying to find its owner.

I made my living by feeling others' pain, mostly animals. I would let my hand go intuitively to the area of pain like a magnet to a piece of steel. For years in my practice I would regularly find the same particular pattern of injury on many different animals. It was a healer's journey of learning that particular "injury of the year." I always ended up with the same malady myself, which was the ultimate teaching in deep physical empathy and genuine understanding. This sticky journey launched me deeper into healing work that required energetic, emotional, and physical boundaries.

In my healer's journey, I also learned about the power of stillness around animals. Stillness holds energy, mystery, richness. Stillness can also release energy. I'm still fascinated by stillness that can transform—like the Water element shapeshifter—into healing.

Water elements also love to dabble in transitions, like the human equivalent of liquid to ice, snow, to steam, and the extremes of hot and cold. Life is our practice field for transformation. We change like the metaphoric water we are, transformed by engagement with the other elements. We often walk between the worlds of Body and Spirit.

My talented friend and colleague Susan Tenney of Elemental Acupressure is a thirty-year practitioner and dynamic international instructor of animal acupressure. One of her fun teachings is "Think of the four elements Wood, Fire, Earth, and Metal as being muggles, and Water is the wizard." That about says it all!

Water elements are guided by ancestral wisdom that often takes a lifetime to recognize, listen to, honor, and utilize. We listen deeply to both worlds and feel even deeper into this world. Curiosity is our friend. Perhaps fear is meant to be too.

	Water Element Human Quiz
	1 = Never true | 2 = Sometimes true | 3 = Always true
	I can feel and read others' feelings and motives
	I like being anonymous
	I have brilliant large-scale ideas but lack the ability to make them happen alone
	I am a starter, not a finisher
	I am extremely curious about many things that others don't care about
	I do not need a big social life, just a few friends
	I love reading and writing daily
	I don't mind being alone
	My inner world is very complex
	I can communicate with the beyond and different realms when I choose
	I go with the flow with most things in life
	I do a lot of self-reflection
	I intuitively shapeshift to other elements with the seasons
	I don't like being disturbed during my creative work
	I often disappear from the world and sometimes do not respond to others' communications
	I am very private
	I can get suspicious of others
	I have strong empathic abilities and am very sensitive to others energy
	I love delving into the mysteries of life
	I strongly appreciate Nature and her power and beauty
	Water Element Total

9. The Weaving of Relationships

*Learning to find the dance that is possible within
a relationship is not a matter of hope or desire.
It is the journey of a lifetime.*

—SUZANNE CLOTHIER

Now let's look at how the Five Elements play out in your relationships, especially your relationship with your dog.

The ancient Chinese believed that we are nature manifested in human form. Thus, we humans are subject to the same cycles, forces, and patterns as those in Nature. Each of the five elements has a unique and special relationship with all the other elements.

As energy flows in the body, mind, and spirit there is a constant interaction between the elements. If one element is out of balance it will eventually create an imbalance in one or all of the elements, bringing on disharmony, and possibly health and behavior issues.

Balance can be created with both simple understanding and supportive elemental tools when dealing with personality and behavioral aspects in our dogs, ourselves, and other humans in our life. Relationship dynamics that are out of balance can be more easily worked with once we understand the element we are dealing with. It takes a bit of effort and retraining but with mindful observation and information we can become wiser in our approaches. Understanding the elemental archetypes in your relationships will help guide the process of balance/imbalance instead of reacting to it. To help understand the movement, dynamics, and effects of elemental change in our relationship dynamics with our dogs and others, we will look at the two guardians of growth and balance: the Sheng (creation) cycle and the Ko (control) cycle.

Figure 13: Sheng and Ko cycles

The Sheng cycle and Ko cycle are known as the "great balancers" for the five elements—Wood, Fire, Earth, Metal, and Water. These two cycles work together and independently to continually adjust and create balance. Each element is part of a continuous transformational cycle within the larger structure of our lives. Creating balance is the way to create health in the body, mind, spirit, and in our relationships.

These two cycles, Sheng and Ko, are primarily used for assessment and treatment in the TCM art of acupressure and acupuncture, diet, lifestyle changes, etc. For our purposes, we are observing how they operate in the elemental archetype relationship between humans and dogs.

Sheng (Creation) Cycle

The creation or Sheng cycle nourishes birth, needed growth, and abundant movement forward. This cycle provides a continuous flow of nourishing energy that moves clockwise around the circle of elements, creating a relationship between each element as it cycles. Notice the directions of the arrows on Figure 14 on the following page.

Figure 14: Sheng creation cycle

- Wood creates Fire: Wood makes fire burn.
- Fire creates Earth: When fire burns it creates ash, which creates earth.
- Earth creates Metal: Earth produces ore/metal.
- Metal creates Water: Water makes condensation on metal.
- Water creates Wood: Water is important to the growth of a tree for wood.

This all sounds wonderful … until it's not! Too much of a "good thing" can be toxic when unchecked. Think about drinking too much caffeine. It makes you feel on top of the world… until it doesn't. Then it results in stomachaches, jitteriness, and lack of sleep.

Sheng (Creation) Cycle Excess Example

Wood elements are structured, disciplined, athletic, competitive, and determined. Wood energy will blend well with a Fire energy as it creates and feeds the fire. But if there is too much Wood the Fire will rage, run wild, tear down structures, and eventually burn itself out. Consider the following scenario illustrating an excess creation cycle between a dog and its human: A Wood owner demands too much training, structure, working time, and competition of a Fire Dog who truly just loves fun, play, socializing, being touched, and loved. Fire Dog is trying extra hard to please the Wood owner but can't quite hack the disciplined structure. Fire Dog begins to have regular panic attacks (disturbance of the Shen) and the Wood owner gets upset and thinks more structure and training will help, eventually burning out the Fire Dog who becomes anxiety ridden, shows destructive and bizarre behavior, loses self-confidence, begins excessive barking, and eventually gets moved on and rehomed.

If there is too much growth (too much Wood feeding the Fire) in each element a potentially harmful imbalance could reel out of control, carrying too much power and ultimately doing harm.

Ko (Control) Cycle

The control or Ko cycle puts the brakes on and tempers the over-exuberant creation cycle. This cycle also occurs innately in nature. It is the cycle of control and destruction, of checks and balances. We can see the Ko cycle in the natural world as it constantly interacts to restore balance. Wood and falling logs can slow the erosion of earth's movement by holding back and shaping the earth to hold steady while the live tree's roots create a web of strength and structure for the earth and all it feeds, gifts, and houses within. Fire softens and tempers metal to shape it into tools, vessels, unique inventions, tiny fittings to hold our lives together. These Metal objects are then used as tools to make wood into objects of necessity for our purposes and also to create healthy forests that continue to feed the earth and its inhabitants. Earth dams up, slows down, and creates direction for Water. Water quiets the excesses of Fire, and feeds and replenishes what Fire has damaged.

What the natural world creates, can always be altered or destroyed. Nature has her innate checks and balances. The Ko cycle works to create balance and harmony for the unchecked creation cycle.

Notice arrow directions on Figure 15 on the following page.

Figure 15: Ko control cycle

- Wood controls Earth – Wood can shape and hold earth from moving.
- Earth controls Water – Earthen dams can stop the flow of water.
- Water controls Fire – Water can extinguish fire.
- Fire controls Metal – Fire melts metal, tempers it, and makes it shapeable.
- Metal controls Wood – Metal saws can cut trees and shape wood.

Ko (Control) Cycle Example

Let's continue with the scenario of the Wood owner who can't cope with the Fire Dog. A human Water element now adopts the Fire Dog and calmly puts out the raging fire in its burned-out, panic-stricken heart. Water partner softens this disturbance of the Shen with patience, acceptance, compassion, and kindness and the Fire Dog's very favorite things—adoration, praise, and fun. The Water partner, who has had other rescues, has great empathy for those who have been misunderstood and just need some love to be the very best version of themselves. Fire Dog and Water partner hang out and cuddle together and walk the neighborhood saying hello to everyone. Fire Dog gets to go everywhere in the car with Water partner; they play, nap, and go camping at lakes together. There they meet other dogs and people and have cozy campfires. Life is good, balance is better.

Creation vs. Control

Conversely, the Creation cycle also restores balance when the Control cycle is out of control. Give and take, yin and yang, light and dark—each cooperates to maintain an earthly balance in Mother Nature and in our natures.

Here is an example of the Creation cycle in action:

Mr. Metal lives his life being purposeful, intense, and driven to fix things and make the world a better place. He is so focused on his work that he frequently exhausts himself. Yet he cannot rest and fun is never on his radar. Mr. Metal has an Earth Dog who is sweet, a bit lazy, social, and loves treats. Earth Dog is faithful and devoted to Mr. Metal and follows him everywhere. This has been a somewhat challenging relationship mix for both Mr. Metal and Earth Dog, with Mr. Metal always moving and working, and Earth Dog just wanting some lazy time in the sun. One day Mr. Metal physically crashes from overwork and is forced to take a sabbatical. Earth Dog sees his chance (enter Creation cycle).

Earth Dog finally gets to share his desire for true companionship and laziness, and is able to give some nurturing kindness to Mr. Metal. He curls up and cuddles with Mr. Metal as he rests and watches over him each day, reminding him where the treat jar is on a regular basis. When Mr. Metal awakes, Earth Dog wags and wiggles while bringing toys and dirty socks to Mr. Metal. One day he finally makes Mr. Metal smile again and suddenly Mr. Metal notices the Earth Dog's grounded, caring presence and genuine concern. This touches Mr. Metal's heart and he wonders how he missed this precious kindness for so long in his Earth Dog partner. When the time is right Earth Dog runs over and gets his leash and hands it to Mr. Metal which makes him laugh, something this Metal human hasn't done in a long time.

Off they go on a walk outside together, with Earth Dog as envoy in the lead saying hello to all the neighbors and forcing Mr. Metal to actually socialize, which Mr. Metal realizes he awkwardly enjoys. Life is good, balance is better.

This is the relationship aspect of the Sheng or Creation cycle in action. Too much controlling and fixing for the overworked Metal (excess control or Ko) and in steps supportive Earth, which in the Creation cycle elementally feeds and holds space for Metal while balancing the rhythms and potential of Metal.

These cycles of relationships weave in and out of our lives on a regular basis. We may never notice them but when unchecked for too long they can create disharmony in the body, mind, and spirit. There are many combinations of cycle balancing that can be seen in life and our relationships with our dogs; all it takes is a little observation. Always remember that we are all five elements so look to your quiz results for each element to determine the other factors affecting "who they are" and "who you are." There is an infinite number of combinations!

In the Five Element relationship system, there are no "bad" relationships. All relationships inherently allow you to expand your skills of understanding, acceptance, empathy, listening, and compassion. Relationships are your guidebook to achieving harmony within yourself. The relationship challenges are your practice field for better understanding yourself and your reactions to others. The connection point is where the magic begins!

10. Balancing and Blending for Harmony

Being happy never goes out of style.
—LILY PULITZER

Balancing Acts

It can be difficult to stay balanced on a daily basis, all the time. That is one of our biggest human challenges in life from beginning to end. I truly think the animals are more talented at this juggling act than we humans.

As humans, we often have so many things flying about in our lives. Some of these things can tip our sensitive scales if we are not truly listening to our inner selves. Or we are not doing the supportive self-care techniques that our element needs. The support tools for the dog elements are the same for the human elements. As you navigate your own primary element, be sure to reference the wants and needs and supportive techniques in the dog element chapters and use them as your own human elemental self-care bundle. Remember, the elemental concepts are the same for dogs and humans, just the life applications are different.

We also have the responsibility of managing and balancing our dog's lives for their well-being and happiness. The lives of our dogs are more controlled in terms of stimulus, opportunity, and even simple choices like eating and going potty. When these activities are unregulated or randomly managed, we can cause huge disharmonies in our animals and often within ourselves. For example, my dogs Wilbur and Pretzel know exactly what time they are fed, as did all of the many other animals in my life. They gently and somewhat politely remind me if I'm off schedule feeding. (Particularly good at this are the Earth animals.) They also ask—and I listen—when they need to go potty. This creates an adaptive communication between us and allows them some control over their lives, which reduces stress for all of us.

Be kind and consistent, and keep an open connection with your four-legged partners. They give us so much heart, love, and laughter and deserve to live a balanced, harmonious life, just as we do.

For us to create balance and harmony in relationship with our dog or others, we need to be sure that one or preferably both of us participating in that relationship is balanced in their own element. Animals and some humans may be patient with us when we are not in a balanced state, however some may not. Human and dog Earth elements have eternal patience but also a perfect clock and are easily upset with lack of routine. Fires are always sincerely interested in helping you rebalance with some laughter and fun, and although they need some routine they can happily live with the whims of their human's balance or rebalance. Water is very empathetic and will feel and understand your lack of balance but will also develop their own internal stress as they take on your life imbalance and stressors. Wood is not very tolerant of imbalance, nor is Metal. Wood will get impatient and Metal will lose trust and faith in you as a human caregiver and partner.

The bottom line is that one of you in the relationship—either animal or human—should be in a balanced state to guide the other back into harmony and balance, both within yourselves and within your relationship. Dogs, living so closely with humans for so many centuries, often innately know how to fix us if we just listen and let them. When your dog really wants to go out for a walkie, listen to them. It is probably not at all about them but perhaps something they are seeing in you. After some fresh air you will probably come back feeling some contentment and balance again.

By following the Five Element suggestions in preceding chapters, we now know some simple ways to help rebalance the dog and ourselves. It may also take a small village of acupuncturists, acupressure practitioners, bodyworkers, trainers, and veterinarians to fully bring about the rebalancing act. The same is needed for us humans—except maybe the veterinarian! Be sensitive, observant, and caring. Check in often on the balance ratio of both of you for the best relationship success. Sometimes rebalancing the dog rebalances ourselves. And sometimes rebalancing ourselves rebalances the dogs. Life is good, balance is better.

The following pages will give you some baseline information for blending the primary elements together and creating a healthy, gratifying relationship. Remember that there are no "bad" relationships that we need to avoid due to your primary element type or another's primary element type. It is up to us to expand our skills of self-awareness, listening, and communication, and make healthy decisions about our interactions and reactions. Becoming a better partner to any of the elements while remaining true to ourselves can create the balance and harmony we strive for in our daily lives.

Extroverts, Introverts, and Energy

There are numerous ways to consider the relationships between two elements. Some elements are extroverts and some introverts by nature. This often correlates with the "speed" at which each element moves through daily life and how they react to stress. Extrovert elements tend to get along better with other extrovert elements. Introverts and Introverts also may do well together. Earth is in the middle world and is happiest if someone just has snacks!

Social traits of the elemental personalities

Wood	Extrovert	Likes stimulus and doing, quick reflexes under stress
Fire	Extrovert	Does not like being alone, hyper under stress or too much excitement
Earth	In the middle	Likes routine, calm and slower in life, worries under stress
Metal	Introvert	Quiet, calm, focused, aloof under stress
Water	Introvert	Sensitive to environment, emotions, fearful under stress

With so many distinctively unique combinations of elements it can seem daunting to hone in on the advantages and the triggers that are in play for you and your dog. But, it's easy! Just be sure to focus on your dog's and your own "primary" elements first. You can easily work with those to tailor your relationship. Eventually you'll begin to expand your relationship and notice the second and third elements of you both and even figure in where and when you might see the fourth and fifth element showing up.

Element Combinations and How They Work Together

Wood and Wood: good mix

Upside: A great combination when they are balanced. They like the same things, can challenge each other, usually have similar drive and determination.

Downside: Sometimes there is an issue with leadership so a friendly competitive challenge can turn into a leadership challenge as well. This is more common with human/human relationships. Also, if there is a relationship imbalance, anger can arise. Two angry, warring Woods is not a pretty sight, nor does it usually resolve or end well. It can be messy!

Wood and Fire: can be good

Upside: There is always a clear leader and that is usually the Wood, hopefully a balanced Wood. Both have high energy. A balanced Wood can keep a Fire focused and know when "too much is too much" for them. Fires can soften Wood's seriousness and convince them to have some fun.

Downside: Woods are clear, determined, and focused. Fires can have attention issues and nervousness, and may want to play hard but not work hard. Fires can often be ungrounded while Wood is very grounded.

Wood and Earth: not so good

Upside: Earth is very supportive and nurturing for Wood (who may not want to be nurtured).

Downside: Earth is a much slower paced being, and Wood can get frustrated with that. Wood is much more athletic and determined than Earth. Earth has very different and more relaxed priorities than Wood.

Wood and Metal: good combination!

Upside: Wood respects a balanced Metal and vice versa. Both have high energy. Both are very capable. They can make a great team.

Downside: Minor, but Wood is competitive while Metal is purpose driven.

Wood and Water: can be good

Upside: Water gives Wood growth. Wood respects the quiet strength of Water. Wood can dam up Water and create stillness for Water when it is flowing too much. Water can easily mask Wood when needed.

Downside: Energy levels are generally polar opposites: think winter's quiet (Water) vs. spring's burgeoning growth (Wood).

Fire and Fire: fun!

Upside: Both high energy, stimulus craving, fun loving, social, and party divas. Both lightworkers spreading goodness to everyone and everything.

Downside: Both can burn out, have panic attacks, unground regularly, and spiral into Shen disturbances. Then who supports whom?

Fire and Earth: good!

Upside: Both are very heart-centered, caring elements. Both like play more than work.

Downside: Energy levels are different but Fire can motivate Earth and Earth can relax Fire.

Fire and Metal: okay, sometimes

Upside: Fire controls and tempers Metal's rigidity and asks Metal not to be so inflexible. Fire wants Metal to step out and have some fun—not always easy! But Fire can have the gentle upper hand, thanks to its position in the Ko cycle.

Downside: Metal needs quietness and correctness in life and Fire wants stimulus, whimsy, and can turn incorrectness into fun which may or may not work with Metal.

Fire and Water: strangely good, except when it's not

Upside: Fire's warmth and heart-centered liveliness can warm Waters affection and open up a desire to connect. Fire is like a lighted buoy for Water's quiet depths. Water controls Fire so there is usually no fear within these relationships.

Downside: Water can extinguish Fire's liveliness (Ko), Fire can become bored with Water's depth of thinking and feeling.

Earth and Wood: not so good

Upside: Earth is very supportive and nurturing for Wood. Earth can make slow steady progress towards goals while Wood's goals are much higher and more persistent and often urgent.

Downside: Earth is a much slower paced being, and Wood can get frustrated with that. Wood is much more athletic and determined than Earth.

Earth and Earth: good

Upside: Earths will understand and appreciate each other and will bask in the simplicity of life together. They have similar goals which are not always lofty but important in an earthly grounded way. They will nurture each other and everything around them.

Downside: Two Earths together can tend towards laziness, indulging in too many yummy snacks with a primary goal of enjoying all their favorite things which may be wonderful, until it's not! This may create imbalances in their health. When food means love, such as too many treats for the dog, this can create health issues.

Earth and Metal: not a great mix

Upside: Earth wants to relax while supporting Metal's busyness. Metal wants to do, plan, and accomplish, and will appreciate Earth's support.

Downside: Strong conflict in energy and emotional flexibility levels.

Earth and Water: good

Upside: Earth is a great listener and will appreciate Water's in-depth view of life. Earth is easy going and Water often goes with the flow. Earth can dam up Water when they are flowing too much, and provide boundaries that are appreciated and helpful to Water.

Downside: Earth worries and Water has fear, not always the best combination for any life challenges. Water can sense and feel Earth's worry and turn it into fear. Earth can also move slowly on decisions and changes, while Water is incredibly swift and adaptive and can transform and adjust to new circumstances quickly. Water's shapeshifting may make Earth's steady-minded and routine-based head spin.

Metal and Wood: good combination!

Upside: Wood respects a balanced Metal and vice versa, both have high energy, both are very capable and forward moving.

Downside: Minor, but Wood is competitive while Metal is purpose driven.

Metal and Metal: almost great mix

Upside: Two Metals can change the world with their purpose-driven attributes, brilliant minds, and high energy. They are an excellent working team.

Downside: Two Metals can easily clash due to their tendency towards inflexibility. These standoffs may never be resolved. If there is a loss of a loved one or circumstance, they may not be able to get past it and may spend their lives in a constant state of grief.

Metal and Water: good mix

Upside: Metal can appreciate the complex mind and spirit of Water. Metal creates Water and can deeply understand and empathize with Water's need for both movement and stillness. Although they think in different ways they fill in for each other and blend together a whole train of thoughts and feelings—on life and the otherworldly realms. Metal will fill in some parameters for Water's creativity on projects and correct issues where needed.

Downside: Metal may move too fast and be too purpose driven to take time for Water's emotional needs.

Water and Water: hmmm

Upside: Mutual deep understanding and acceptance for each other. Powerful spirits that may spend a lot of time debating deep life questions. Both can communicate in different realms and often do. Feel a sense of belonging when together.

Downside: Can drown each other in strange physical issues, and deep fear or lack of fear. Can have turbulent emotions within the relationship.

Like Attracts Like

Lastly, you may notice that often "like attracts like." This pairing can be extremely beneficial in understanding the individual elements themselves. Perhaps the attraction is the uncomplicated familiarity and magnetic understanding one feels when they meet another of their element clan. The elemental energies can automatically blend with each other, creating a depth of understanding that initially unites the two. Just remember we all have unique combinations of "five" elements. Those will determine how the actual relationship ultimately works once the attraction wears off.

Fire, Earth, and Water elements tend to attract the same element. They are all concerned with comfort and interaction with others. Fires are very social, curious, and have dynamic, fun personalities. Earths are gentle caregivers interested in the well-being of others and automatically liking nearly everyone they meet. Waters are often quiet but intrigued by fun, dynamic, and caring people and new interesting topics. You can see how these three elements could attract each other like magnets. Wood elements are fairly competitive with other Woods. Metals can be rigid in their opinions and more solitary.

Wood and Metal elements can be great combinations of the same element but when they are imbalanced, cannot always overcome the hurdles. An inner sense may be warning them about this.

Wood and Wood will attract each other but for innately competitive reasons. It is their true nature. They compete on levels that they may not even be aware of. Combine that with strong leadership roles and two Wood elements can either clash or build healthy respect for one another.

Metals are strong and determined in their purpose, and when a balanced Metal meets another balanced Metal or Wood, together they can change the world.

When like attracts like, it can easily exacerbate certain traits of the elements. This can be either harmonious—as for Fire, Earth, and Water— or tumultuous—as for Wood and Metal. Pretzel and I are both primary Water Elements. We both shapeshift regularly and have developed a respect for each other no matter who we are at any given moment. It's summer, Fire element season, and we are having lots of fun play together along with Wilbur and his secondary Fire element! Soon we will all three transition to Earth, slow down a bit, and eat yummy snacks while earthing!

Strategies for Rebalancing – Bringing Calmness and Clear Focus to Each Element

Something that is important for each elemental relationship is knowing what gives both you and your dog peace, calmness, and clear focus. These are important approaches, specific to each element, for creating peace within your partner and your relationship. Utilizing these strategies at just the right time can get you out of an active stress situation or a chronic stress or imbalance with each other. These simple approaches can shift things back to a balanced state before they become a runaway train.

Strategies for rebalancing

Wood	Movement, learning, purpose
Fire	Grounded fun things, adoration, connection with others, touch
Earth	Comfort foods, relaxing together, slowing down, earthing
Metal	Quiet, meditation, peacefulness, clarity, purpose, learning, yoga
Water	Connection, nature time, noticing beauty, stillness, good sleep, naps

Even if you think you are balanced, be sure to regularly utilize these calming and focus tools for yourself, as well as the other animal or person you are interacting with.

There may, however, be times when you are unable to use these methods with others. This is when you really need to create a solid, focused balance and resilience within yourself. We often can't or choose not to see our own imbalances clearly. The self-care analogy most often used is we must put on our oxygen masks first before helping others. Time to turn on the self-awareness switch and utilize what you instinctively know about your own elemental constitution. Using these simple but profound tools during challenging times—illness, injury, disharmony, lack of connection, aging animals and humans, high stress—can cultivate a strong sense of well-being and overall balanced quality of life.

These simple aids, used on a regular basis, can internally, externally, and energetically refresh us and our relationships quickly. Practice becoming the best version of you and you will create and maintain more compassionate and successful relationships and in doing so will grow the fruits of health and harmony for our beloved dogs and the world around you.

Life is good, balance is better!

11. Rescue and Shelter
Applications of
Five Element Theory

You can't change a dog's past,
but you can rewrite their future.
—AGNES CARASS

One of my long-term life visions has been to see this amazing ancient wisdom help rescued animals and rescue workers as they intertwine during capture situations, in kennels, and during long-term kennel stays.

There are countless applications for the personality aspects of the Five Element theory in the dog rescue, shelter, and animal welfare world. As animal welfare professionals strive for ease of connection while they acquire animals, handle and manage them, and foster successful relationships when the animal finds a home, the five elements can come to the rescue . . . literally!

This program sheds a new light on how professionals and dog owners see the animals they work with in the field, during disasters, in kennels, homes, and rehabilitation programs. The Five Element theory fosters a unique approach to the animal's well-being during these processes. It cultivates understanding, patience, empathy, and compassion within our dog/human interactions and relationships.

This simple, highly effective wisdom can easily be integrated into most shelter programs, activities, and lifestyles. It can help create effective protocols and care designed to meet each individual rescue dog's elemental needs, while creating clearer relationships between the handlers and animals. The five elements will help rescue personnel understand why different dogs do different things when under stress. It can also help handlers and new owners understand why dogs won't do what we want them to do. Age-old wisdom for age-old questions!

The five elements explain the five distinct archetypal patterns of behaviors in a way that is easy to learn. Behaviors we may see in our dogs, other animals, colleagues, and ourselves suddenly have a context and a pattern. This interspecies x-ray vision gives us a clear understanding of the five distinct personalities and the specific indicators that steer us toward the rescue dog's predominant elements. It's a practical and easy way to create harmony with our dogs, in both our work and home life.

In addition, the Five Element lens can also help us humans find our own elements and create even better overall relationships with our colleagues. This can create powerful understanding and creative team-building opportunities.

The Five Element theory works with specific affiliations and key aspects of each dog element's personality. To effectively assess personality, we look at the following traits for each element: archetypes, emotions, wants, needs, stressors, balancers, and potential strengths and weaknesses. This helps us see how each dog or human element responds to the world around them and why. This is an invaluable perspective to have in the animal welfare world.

Here are some potential rescue dog and shelter applications for this program:

- Clear identification of stress behavior reflex by the first responder to help identify the dog's element profile—how did the dog react during capture?
- Understanding the dog's element can be valuable for selecting calming techniques during handling and exercise time, and overall management in kennels.
- Utilizing Five Element strategies for ways of being and doing that soothe and calm dogs during the rescue process, in shelters, and in their transition to their new home.

- Five element personality assessments can be used to help these animals find the right humans and to transition smoothly into their new home.
- As shelter staff work with the dog and get to know it, Five Element information can act as relationship counseling information and can be given to the new potential owner.
- With a few simple questions on an adopter's application, the perfect elemental dog/human match can be made!
- This program can seamlessly mesh with any existing shelter program.

The Five Element theory is more than just a fun curiosity. It has the potential to change the lives of many animals, both in rescue situations, finding the right homes, and for staying permanently in those homes. Sending home element profile information with a new, excited owner can ease the dog's transition, and create a solid understanding in that happy, forever home that we all desire for these animals.

Animal welfare work is not easy. If we can learn something that softens some of the difficult moments in these situations, then this is all worth it. I know and believe this can create a win-win for saving lives, securing and easing the rescue dog's transition into their new home, and can boost the staying power to keep them there, while easing the trauma, drama, and compassion fatigue that animal welfare workers experience. Isn't that what we all want?

We are all in this together!

I am happy to discuss, guide, and teach any rescue programs about this easy to learn and potentially powerful program—another tool for your toolbox. We can make a difference!

Check out the Resources page 178 for more information.

12. The Happy Wagging Tail
A Love Letter to Dogs

*Money can buy you a fine dog, but only love
can make him wag his tail.*
—KINKY FRIEDMAN

Who doesn't love a happy wagging tail? Animal behaviorists have long since gathered all the clues of tail height, sweep range, and speed that can determine the nuances and meanings of numerous different tail wags, including my favorite—*happy wagging*. Can't you just feel the beautiful energy of *happy* when your pup is happy wagging? Doesn't it just fill you up with a big smile? I've watched stone-faced people soften and break into the most beautiful smile when a happy wagging dog tail says hello. I've spent my whole life trying to make that happen. My own efforts pale compared to my dog's successes!

Truth be told, I've learned from my dogs how to vicariously happy wag my tail when I see a dear friend, or something that touches my heart or makes me laugh. And of course, I always happy wag when I see a happy wagging dog!

I like to think of happy wagging as a sign of connection, a deep, heart-opening connection that floats gratitude all around you like a gentle mist on a hot day. The kind that fills your whole body with an utterly complete smile. To me happy wagging is a metaphor for a peaceful, meaningful existence, one that brings happiness and joy to the little things in life. A wag here, a wag there, look at all the beautiful energy we can toss out into the wind to blow seeds that flower and create more smiles. It truly can be contagious!

We are in a refreshing new era of honoring the silent connections we have with our incredible dogs and all sentient beings here on Earth.

Noticing the complexities of the interweaving of their lives with ours gives us a drive to learn more, and to create space in our hearts to share, advocate, and support their evolution and each being's genuine expression.

Everyone and everything has a purpose, a reason for being. Bees have the amazing job of pollinating plants and making yummy honey in the process. Birds scatter seeds for new growth while giving us beauty and joyful songs. Dogs give us loyalty, laughter, companionship, and if we are listening, teach us about life. How can we be the best expression of ourselves as humans to accomplish what these beings can? How can we open our eyes and hearts to truly see who other beings are, and create a beautiful bubble of understanding that enfolds our relationships? How can we learn from the many, many teachings of all these amazing beings here on earth?

We can widen our view, quiet our minds, and open our hearts to find genuine empathy and awe for every creature, large and small. Like the many great masters before us, we can accept others and their place in the world. We can be a steward for their growth and a vibrant torch for their well-being. We can daily embrace our Five Element wisdom to find the best versions of ourselves and others.

This understanding, compassion, and empathy can be a panacea for our inner selves and our relationships. Animals feel all our vibrations. The tiniest beings, even bugs and plants, and certainly our dogs, can be affected by our inner thoughts and feelings. The more awareness and kindness we project, the more we see and feel kindness.

Dogs are ambassadors for the many other species of this world. They were brave enough many centuries ago to step up and be part of our human lives. I envision that the first humans who accepted dogs as companions felt that happy wagging smile surround them and deeply touch their own wild hearts. I am certain it was an odd feeling but a good one, which has managed to endure and expand for centuries. Dogs too have endured and thrived beside us, as we have beside them. For dogs it is a very long story of leaving the wild behind and moving towards domestication. But the species accomplished it. Now it is time for us to return back to the wild that we once knew and honored. The wild of our hearts.

A dog's medicine is trust, loyalty, reflection, protection, family, honor, and integrity.

These are all solid values that live in the uncharted wilds of our human hearts. Dogs ask us to explore these values within ourselves and walk a good road with each step we take. They are truly our teachers, even when we think we are teaching them.

When we look at the interactive personalities of our dogs and ourselves, our different or similar wants and needs, we can finally understand the unique dynamics that brought us together so many moons ago. Dogs and humans have always shared an innate drive for companionship and family, as well as the need for support and guidance, and if we humans pay attention, we also share our high sensitivity levels for both others, our own health and well-being, and even sometimes, danger.

We can also see the richness, joy, and supportive structures in our combined relationships. This understanding can soften our judgements, stimulate acceptance for who we both are, and create a gentle harmony between us.

Understanding can truly make the world a better place, as our peaceful home vibrations reach out and stretch like the sun to create a kinder, gentler world. Every piece of awareness, acceptance, and clarity fills not only our life but energetically radiates out into the world, making life just a little bit better and a little bit brighter. We finally see the background behind the stage and it's not nearly as scary as we thought it was. It holds whimsy, hope, and potential.

It holds a happy wagging tail.

APPENDIX A

Dog Element Quizzes

When completing each quiz, rate each question from 1 to 3 and then add the total up at the end.

Wood Dog Quiz	
	1 = Never true | 2 = Sometimes true | 3 = Always true
	I am happiest when I get movement each day
	I get impatient when I am learning the same thing over and over
	I often have muscle tightness
	I love to compete
	I am happiest with a structured daily program
	I am not afraid of conflict with other animals or humans
	I have an extremely strong will to succeed
	I am always courageous and never show fear
	I like to know exactly where all my toys, gear, and handler are
	I am highly determined to succeed
	I am hardworking
	I love challenges
	I am incredibly devoted and loyal to my handler
	I will fiercely protect my humans and friends
	I perform very well under stress
	I am confident
	I am a good communicator of my needs or problems
	I notice and don't like bad people
	I can find it difficult to relax or "turn off"
	I want and need a job and am best as a working dog with one partner
	Wood Element Dog Total

Fire Dog Quiz	
1 = Never true | 2 = Sometimes true | 3 = Always true	
	I love all humans and want to be around them
	I wag my whole body incessantly when someone comes to say hi
	I love to be petted and noticed
	I sometimes have separation anxiety when my human leaves
	I love to be petted and always want more
	I treat everyone like I've known them forever
	I need to feel loved at all times, feeling loved makes me feel safe
	I can be a bit of a ham and want to be adored by everyone
	I'm smart but have trouble focusing for too long when new people or friends are around
	I can get overexcited and turn into a drama queen
	People get happy when they meet me or visit with me
	I enjoy being social with other dogs and want to visit or play with everyone
	When I have too much fun I can panic and get confused
	I overheat easily even when it's not summer
	I can become nervous or full of anxiety if things aren't "normal"
	When I feel stressed I can panic and completely unground
	I can become hypersensitive to foods/lotions/potions and meds
	I bark a lot
	I lick a lot
	I love to cuddle
	Fire Element Dog Total

Earth Dog Quiz	
1 = Never true | 2 = Sometimes true | 3 = Always true	
	I love having children or other pets around me
	I love meeting new people
	I am very loyal to my family
	I love having company visit, both animals and humans
	I get very worried when things change in my household
	I worry and obsess when my food is late
	I do not like suitcases
	I get confused with too much training or too many requests
	I never forget a face or place
	I protect my family especially the little ones
	I sashay when I walk while my tail wags a lot
	I love quiet time with my special person
	I LOVE TREATS and ask for them regularly
	I get very stressed and go flat and hide when people argue or yell
	I love to snuggle with anyone and everyone
	I'm not very competitive
	I share my toys and bed
	I take on my human's stress
	I can be overprotective
	I gain weight easily
	Earth Element Dog Total

Metal Dog Quiz	
1 = Never true | 2 = Sometimes true | 3 = Always true	
	With a competent, correct, and fair handler I am intelligent and a fast learner
	I learn best with a systematic approach
	I avoid conflict
	I am polite around people and other dogs
	I can be stand-offish with both dogs and humans
	I don't really need touch and cuddles
	I don't get overly excited about things in my environment
	I am pretty quiet and don't bark very often
	I tend to be lean and graze my food
	I glide when I walk or run and have good dog posture
	I don't really act crazy or have fun like other dogs
	I love and need to have a purpose
	I grieve when I lose a friend, a job, or one of my people
	I prefer one-on-one relationships
	I don't often play with toys
	I follow all house rules
	I am very patient
	I isolate myself for rest time
	I don't like chaos
	It takes me time to trust someone
	Metal Element Dog Total

Water Dog Quiz
1 = Never true | 2 = Sometimes true | 3 = Always true
I am not very sociable with other dogs or humans
I tend to retreat within myself for safety and rest
I am wary of humans and their motives
I am very curious about bugs, smells, people's skin, toes, socks, birds, new household items
I often hide behind my handler when in groups
I love learning new things
I have a complex inner and lively self that I only show to my close handler or partner
I am happy to follow and not lead
I am playful when I feel loved
I want someone to love and understand me
I can be persistent
I am easygoing with changes in routine
I can fall into visceral fear easily or be completely fearless, to my disadvantage
It takes me time to trust someone
My movement flows like water
I speak a lot and am a good clear communicator in other ways
I can be suspicious of humans
I never forget past hurts and pains
I can easily change elements to suit the circumstance
Home is my safe haven
Water Element Dog Total

APPENDIX B
Human Element Quizzes

When completing each quiz, rate each question from 1 to 3 and then add the total up at the end.

Wood Element Human Quiz	
	1 = Never true | 2 = Sometimes true | 3 = Always true
	I am courageous and determined in life
	I don't change my mind easily once I make a decision
	I am honest and dependable
	I love to compete
	I have intense focus
	I like to be in charge or a leader and will naturally fill that void if there is one
	I can reflex to anger, impatience, frustration
	I have strong personal boundaries
	I do not like having my time wasted by someone
	I perform well and sometimes my best, under stress
	I am a very good and effective communicator
	I am a hard worker and expect the same from others
	I can be critical or judgmental
	It's hard for me to delegate
	I have a hard time relaxing
	I can be compassionate and very generous when there is a need
	I can lose my temper easily
	I love challenges and thrive to succeed in life
	I love to exercise and do challenging sports
	I want control over all things in my life
	Wood Element Total

	Fire Element Human Quiz
	1 = Never true | 2 = Sometimes true | 3 = Always true
	I love stimulating environments
	I often feel joy and try to spread it around to others
	I love being the life of the party
	I like people and love being around others
	I love to dance and laugh and have fun
	I feel others' emotions and try to help cheer them up when they need it
	I love telling stories and tend to exaggerate a bit just for fun
	I am an optimist at heart even when things aren't going well
	I can panic easily
	I can lapse into periods of anxiety
	My heart can range from broken to exhilarated in moments
	I like to move and am not good at sitting very long
	I love high energy exercise classes
	I love meeting new people
	People tell me I smile through my words
	I love making people smile
	I can easily get scatterbrained and disorganized
	My attention hops around and I can have trouble staying focused
	I have a hard time saying no
	I can exhaust myself from too much fun
	Fire Element Total

Earth Element Human Quiz	
1 = Never true | 2 = Sometimes true | 3 = Always true	
	I love spending time with my family
	I love having children and animals around me
	I love supporting others
	I am always available for my friends when they need me
	I feel deep compassion and empathy for others
	I will go out of my way to help others
	I am very loyal
	I don't like change
	I worry a lot
	I sometimes obsessively worry
	I sometimes get obsessive with food
	I love to hug and people love my hugs
	I love to nurture
	I want my home and personality to be comfortable for everyone
	I like non-competitive group exercise
	I don't easily share my problems with others
	I can be stubborn
	I can be overprotective
	I can gain weight easily
	I love sugar and carbohydrates
	Earth Element Human Total

Metal Element Human Quiz	
1 = Never true | 2 = Sometimes true | 3 = Always true	
	I am polite with others
	I do not show emotion when presenting my opinions to others
	I am an intellectual avidly pursuing my own interests
	I try to fix what others don't notice needs fixing
	My personal standards are very high
	I avoid conflict
	I am really not very good at having fun but prefer doing something intellectual instead
	I always try to control my environment
	I don't need many possessions in life
	Food is secondary to work or learning
	I crave solitude and quiet during my down time
	I typically speak softly and with detail
	I exercise with yoga, tai chi, and purposeful movement
	I need a purposeful direction in life and will create one if there isn't one
	I have very good posture
	I tend to isolate myself from humans
	I can be insensitive to others
	I over-analyze almost everything
	I am aloof and become emotionally rigid under stress
	I grieve inwardly for long periods from loss and extreme changes
	Metal Element Total

Water Element Human Quiz	
1 = Never true | 2 = Sometimes true | 3 = Always true	
	I can feel and read others' feelings and motives
	I like being anonymous
	I have brilliant large-scale ideas but lack the ability to make them happen alone
	I am a starter, not a finisher
	I am extremely curious about many things that others don't care about
	I do not need a big social life, just a few friends
	I love reading and writing daily
	I don't mind being alone
	My inner world is very complex
	I can communicate with the beyond and different realms when I choose
	I go with the flow with most things in life
	I do a lot of self-reflection
	I intuitively shapeshift to other elements with the seasons
	I don't like being disturbed during my creative work
	I often disappear from the world and sometimes do not respond to others' communications
	I am very private
	I can get suspicious of others
	I have strong empathic abilities and am very sensitive to others energy
	I love delving into the mysteries of life
	I strongly appreciate Nature and her power and beauty
	Water Element Total

APPENDIX C
Element Dog Overviews

Table 2. Quick reference guide for the five dog elements

Element	Archetype	Strength	Emotion	Season	Sense	Color	Issues	Needs	Stressors
WOOD	Competitor Army sergeant	Athletic Competitive	Anger	Spring	Sight	Black/ brown	Sinews Eyes	Movement	Lack of movement
FIRE	Party dog Diva	Social Friendly	Excess joy Shen	Summer	Speech	Red/white	Heart Heat Skin Stomach	Adoration Social	Chaos Alone Heat
EARTH	Caregiver	Kind Gentle Patient	Worry	Late summer	Taste	Yellow/tan Chubby	Digestive Weight Dental	Food! Routine Family	Off routine Alone
METAL	Librarian	Intelligent Sensitive Focused	Grief	Autumn	Smell	Grey Lean & Muscular	Skin Immune Respiratory	Work Quiet	Noise Losses
WATER	Empath	Sensitive Empathic Wise	Fear	Winter	Hearing	Black mix	Joints Kidney Bladder	Quiet Deep Connection	Chaos Envirotoxins Loud noises

NOTE: This is an abbreviated standard assessment framework for TCM's Five Element theory for dogs. This table is based on personality assessment with a few standard aspects that are important for discovering your dog's element. The extensive standard traditional framework (not shown here) gives TCM practitioners a roadmap to follow for acupuncture, acupressure, diet, and husbandry treatment protocols, which are not in the scope of this book.

Wood Element Dogs

Personality characteristics and support for well-being and balance

Archetype	Army sergeant or upper-level competitor
Strengths	Athletic, competitive, leader, fast learner, benevolent
Emotional default	Anger, frustration, aggression, impatience
Season	Spring
Organs	Gallbladder, liver
Time	11:00 p.m. – 1:00 a.m. and 1:00 a.m. – 3:00 a.m.
Sense organ	Eyes
Sense	Sight
Coat color	Often brown and black
Common issues	Tendon and ligament issues, eye issues, muscle tension
Wants	Movement, variety, competition
Needs	Clear boundaries from human partner, movement, variety, challenge, gentle kindness and appreciation
Stressors	Inconsistent rules and boundaries, boredom
Response to stress	Frustration, impatience, anger
Stress balancers	Consistent boundaries, clear leadership, challenging and varied work, gentle kindness and soft praise
Supportive therapies	Massage, acupressure, swimming, movement, adjunct herbal support
Relationship support	Stay present, clear-headed, and fully engaged when working with Wood Dogs. Maintain solid boundaries and competent, kind leadership. *Do not use force; it will backfire on you!*

Fire Element Dogs

Personality characteristics and support for well-being and balance

Archetype	Party Animal, Diva
Strengths	Charismatic magnetism, friendly, social, playful, fast learner, loves attention and to be adored
Emotional default	Ungrounded, reactivity, disturbance of the Shen
Season	Summer
Organs	Heart, small intestine, pericardium, triple heater
Time	11:00 a.m. – 3:00 p.m. and 7:00 p.m. – 11:00 p.m.
Sense organ	Tongue (licking)
Sense	Speech (barking)
Coat color	Often red or red and white
Common issues	Skin disorders, nervous stomach, heat issues, inflammation
Wants	Play, social stimulation, adoration, cuddles
Needs	Grounded owner, feeling loved, touch, constant emotional connection
Stressors	Overstimulation, busy environments, chaos, being alone or separated from bonded animals or people, heat
Response to stress	Drama queen, stomach upsets, Shen disturbances
Stress support	Physical and emotional contact, attention, fun activities, coolness, soft words and praise, a calm, grounded person or animal
Supportive therapies	Calm touch such as massage and calming acupressure points, cooling foods such as turkey, duck, rabbit, whitefish, cool areas to rest, quiet grounding exercises (ground yourself first!)
Relationship support	Create fun training sessions and be emotionally connected and supportive during training, praise calmly and lavishly! Take them everywhere, especially on your normal routines and walks where they can be adored and feel safe.

Earth Element Dogs

Personality characteristics and support for well-being and balance

Archetype	Quintessential caregiver and nurturer
Strengths	Kind, gentle but brave spirit, patient, loves everyone, loves touch and comfort, dependable, generous, kid-loving, forgiving, great memory, needs routine, with very accurate internal clock
Emotional default	Worry and obsession
Season	Late summer
Organs	Stomach/spleen/pancreas
Time	7:00 a.m. – 11:00 a.m.
Sense organ	Mouth
Sense	Taste
Coat color	Often yellow, tan, or cream or any color that looks chubby
Common issues	Digestive upset, dental issues, growths and fatty tumors, weight gain, gas, bad breath, stifle injuries, hind-end weakness due to weight
Wants	Food, connection, comfort, praise, recognition, love, family
Needs	Routine-based lifestyle, touch, peaceful home atmosphere, food!
Stressors	Lack of routine, complicated requests, expectations of mental quickness
Response to stress	Worry, stubbornness, obsessiveness, lack of confidence, apathy
Stress balancers	Touch, sincere praise, slow fun activities, peaceful environment, comfort, animal and children buddies, weight management
Supportive therapies	Touch, diet considerations, low household stress, regular routine of exercise, herbs or enzymes for digestion, belly lifts for strengthening the back, massage, family, LOVE
Relationship support	Be supportive and patient with slow and steady steps towards a lifetime of dependability and love

Metal Element Dogs
Personality characteristics and support for well-being and balance

Archetype	The Librarian
Strengths	Extremely intelligent, methodical, sensitive, clear-minded focus
Emotional default	Grief
Season	Autumn
Organs	Lung and large intestine
Time	3:00 a.m. – 7:00 a.m.
Sense organ	Nose
Sense	Smell
Coat color	Often grey, white, tan, or rusty, and lean and muscular
Common issues	Skin, respiratory and leg issues, constipation, immune issues
Wants	To work, to have a purpose, to be respected, to trust handler
Needs	Work, purpose, quiet and calm atmosphere for both work and recovery, clear and concise training and communication
Stressors	Commotion, noise, sentimentality, touch, loss of a bonded handler or animal or job
Response to stress	Internalizes stress, impatience, irritation, grief, emotional withdrawal, coughing, skin issues, physical, mental, and emotional rigidity
Stress balancers	Quiet time alone, routine, work, a fully present handler or partner
Supportive therapies	Often does not desire touch but in time can be coaxed to accept it, including acupressure or energy work. Quiet space to recover without noise or chaos. Doggie yoga for flexibility.
Relationship support	Earn his respect and trust by being clear and competent with your training and direction. Bonds deeply to a person he trusts and respects, and will be extremely loyal.

Water Element Dogs

Personality characteristics and support for well-being and balance

Archetype	The Empathic One (four-legged spiritual teacher)
Strengths	Extremely sensitive, deep, wise, quirky, devoted, mystical, emotional, a teacher and guide, pool of reflection for us
Emotional default	Fear
Season	Winter
Organs	Kidney/bladder
Time	3:00 p.m. – 7:00 p.m.
Sense organ	Ears
Sense	Hearing
Coat color	Often all black, or black/white or black/brown
Common issues	Bone and joint issues, bladder, kidney, fertility, thyroid
Wants	Connection, trust, peace, evolution of their human in all ways
Needs	Quiet and peace, safety, deep connection with their human
Stressors	Emotional insensitivity and dishonesty, chaos, loud noises, energetic influences like pesticides, chemical shampoos or cleaners, and power lines
Response to stress	Strange behavior, odd physical ailments, panic
Stress balancers	Maintaining a deep and intimate connection with their human, emotional honesty, rest, elimination of energetic disruptions
Supportive therapies	Energy healing such as Reiki, acupressure, help from animal communicators, herbal/homeopathic/Bach flower remedies
Relationship support	Trust and accept her as your teacher and guide

Resources and Recommended Reading for Your Journey

I hope you enjoyed the book! So glad you made it back here to get this intriguing question answered and visit everyone.

> **How much water does an elephant drink?**
> According to the International Elephant Foundation, an elephant drinks 25–50 gallons or 100–200 liters of water per day. AND their trunk can hold 2.5 gallons of water!!

In this section you will find support for aspects of this book that you may want to dive deeper into. These resources hold the highest standards in their teachings, helping foster deep, soulful connections with animals, while showing us how to utilize them daily in our lives. I have personally had connections and interactions with nearly every one and have integrated many of their teachings and gifts in both my life and work.

Training, Practitioners, Organizations

4Legged Wellness – Rescue and Shelter Applications of the Five Element Personality Protocols

Simple and effective archetypal tools that cultivate deep understanding, create well-being in the lives of rescue animals and rescue personnel, and foster successful relationships during rehoming. For more contact info@4leggedwellness.com.

Tammy Billups

Tammy is an international Interface healing practitioner, author, educator, and pioneer of the animal–human sacred soul partnership. She is the creator of animal–human Tandem Healings™. Her Masterclass courses are deep and refreshing, adding depth to the human–animal relationship. Tammy has a heart as wide as the world. Visit her website for free guided meditations, classes, books, and media presentations: **www.tammybillups.com.**

C.A.L.M. – Conscious Animal Lovers Movement

Alan Schoen, DVM, MS, Ph.D. (hon.), CVA

A note from Dr. Schoen: "Elizabeth's Five Element approach is totally synergistic with the approaches I offer in my online course on C.A.L.M. C.A.L.M. is a culmination of over forty years of my pioneering alternative veterinary medicine career. It is a combination of diverse techniques I have taught in courses and retreats for decades. One goal of C.A.L.M. is to empower animal lovers to care for their animal families at home and prevent problems before they occur. Another goal is to create a global community of conscious animal lovers to discuss subjects regarding how they deepened their relationship with animals. This includes dogs, as well as cats, horses, birds, farm animals, and wildlife. I find this to be essential for us to develop new ways of listening to our hearts' inner guidance and respond to the outer world with a more open mind and heart. The vision of C.A.L.M. is to create a happier, healthier, more harmonious world for all beings. We all know how much this is needed now, more than ever."

More information on **www.drschoen.com.** Dr. Schoen is an accomplished, heartfelt, and delightful author; check out his numerous books.

Caninology and Equinology – Debranne Patillo EEBW

Live and online certification courses covering anatomy, biomechanics, massage, and canine and equine bodywork. Courses are taught both internationally and in the U.S.

Debranne has provided animal bodywork programs for over 30 years, taught by seasoned professionals. These courses are amazing!

See **www.Caninology.com** and **EquinologyInstitute.com.**

Cheryl Schwartz DVM

Dr. Cheryl Schwartz is a holistic veterinarian, author, and educator for over 40 years. She uses a wide range of modalities and is a pioneeer in long-distance animal healing. Dr. Cheryl has helped thousands of animals around the world. Check out her fun classes, videos, books, and acupressure charts at **drcherylschwartz.com**.

Suzanne Clothier

Suzanne Clothier's work reflects a lifetime deeply shared with dogs and animals. She has been working with animals professionally since 1977 with a broad and extensive background of dog training experience. Her Relationship Centered Training (RCT ™) approach has been helping people and dogs around the world for more than 30 years. She is the author of *Bones Would Rain from the Sky*. Check out her training techniques at **www.suzanneclothier.com**; you will find books, online webinars, live classes, DVDs and more.

Elemental Acupressure – Susan Tenney

Awesome training resource for animal acupressure with classes for beginning to advanced practitioners both online and live. Susan is an internationally renowned animal acupressure and shiatsu instructor with 30 years of experience. She is a dynamic, fun, and effective instructor for students at all levels. She has a large international community online that includes her blog, guest bloggers, a book club, as well as many other engaging events and programs. Susan makes acupressure easy and fun for both you and your animals! See **www.elementalacupressure.com** and contact Susan at **info@elementalacupressure.com**.

Joan Ranquet

Joan is an internationally renowned animal communicator, author, educator, and founder of Communication With All Life University. CWALU teaches animal communication and energy healing both live and online. Her courses are engaging and life changing.

Visit her at **www.joanranquet.com**.

Tallgrass Animal Acupressure Resources

Nancy Zidonis and Amy Snow are pioneers in the world of animal acupressure. They are dynamic instructors and authors of numerous animal acupressure books, meridian charts, acupressure apps. You can find out more about their courses, books, and apps at **animalacupressure.com.**

Glacier Peak Holistics

High quality herbal products for dogs and horses. Potent herbal remedies and enzymes for both dogs and horses. See **www.glacierpeakholistics.com.**

Grey Muzzle

The Grey Muzzle Organization improves the lives of at-risk senior dogs by providing funding and resources to animal welfare groups in the U.S. They are the largest nonprofit organization focused specifically on senior dog well-being. They fund medical and dental care, adoptions, hospice, and long-term foster care as well as other special programs for senior dogs. Check out the Resources section on their website, which has a great and informative blog and is chock full of webinars about senior health and well-being, first-aid, alternative care, and end of life care, contributed by many veterinarians, canine therapists, and trainers. It's the most comprehensive library of senior dog information and a great organization to follow and support! Visit **greymuzzle.org.**

Humane Society US

Animal welfare organization focusing on animal protection and ending suffering and animal cruelty in the U.S. **www.humanesociety.org.**

Humane Society International

Works around the globe to protect animals, prevent and confront cruelty, and promote the animal-human bond.

Be sure to check out your local Humane Society in your district for adopting rescues or volunteering! **www.hsi.org.**

Favorite Books on Animals

Acu-Dog: A Guide to Canine Acupressure by Amy Snow and Nancy Zidonis
Animal Soul Contracts by Tammy Billups
Animal Wayshowers by Tammy Billups
Becoming Wild by Carl Safina
Beyond Words by Carl Safina
Dogology by Stefan Gates
Enlightened Dog Training by Jesse Sternberg – also on audio at
   www.peacefulalpha.com
Feeling Grateful by Kobi Yamada
Hope for Animals and Their World by Jane Goodall
Kinship With All Life by J. Allen Boone
Soul Healing with Our Animal Companions by Tammy Billups
The Forever Dog by Rodney Habib & Dr. Karen Shaw Becker
The Other End of the Leash by Patricia B. McConnell, Ph.D.
The Tao of Bow Wow by Deborah Wood
Yin & Yang Nutrition for Dogs by Judy Morgan, DVM and Hue Grant

Books on Five Elements for Humans

The Five Archetypes by Carey Davidson
The Five Element Solution by Jean Haner
The Five Elements by Dondi Dahlin

Acknowledgments

It's amazing as I glance backward at this journey, the many pathways that took me to where I am now, the long gestation culminating in the birth of this book. Among these lighted stepping stones were the gifts of many people sharing their truest feelings thanks to their love for their animals. Thousands of animals with humans that simply wanted to understand and create deeper relationships. Thank you, each one of you for caring enough to share. Many light workers showed up out of the blue and continued to move the idea for this book's pathway forward, some without my knowledge, but all with my immense and humble gratitude.

There was a single moment when the momentum for this book took on a life of its own. Strangely, it started with a stock "paw in a hand" photo that I found. This photo shook my world, and I thought "Aha! The cover of my book!" I searched many book outlets to be sure it wasn't taken… but… it was. A talented healer, teacher, author, and messenger, Tammy Billups, had discovered this soul-reaching photo first. I lost the photo but gained a life-changing, soul-connecting friendship, for which I am beyond grateful. I shared with Tammy a book proposal and partial manuscript and Tammy asked if she could share it with her agent Jon (who I envision as this unknown angel in the background that I hope to meet and personally thank someday). I never did hear from Jon, but he must have seen promise in the idea and unbeknownst to me, handed it off to Sabine Weeke of Findhorn Press/Inner Traditions.

Five months after sending Tammy my proposal, I was contacted by Sabine with an offer of a publishing contract. Thank you, Tammy and Jon!! Sabine is now my guide, my chief hand-holder, and a very supportive and patient wise-woman who gracefully answers all my first-time author questions. Sabine, a kindred lightworker, has the heart and hands of a healer and a deep love for animals. Who better to guide me through the maze of publishing? Many blessings and much gratitude, Sabine!

Alongside Sabine came Jane Ellen Combelic, the amazing editor, animal lover, storyteller, and wisdom keeper who gracefully helped shape my ideas and words in the most beautiful way. Many glorious thanks to you Jane, you are a blessing to my spirit!

Many squishy hugs and mountains of gratitude to Terry Portillo, devoted Sister, and kind, gentle editor. Thank you for always watching my back and tirelessly cheering me on. After reading and cleaning up my rough drafts, you understand my brain better than I do!

I don't know how to express all my gratitude to the amazing team of messengers and caring humans that showed up in so many interesting ways. I can only bow and say an infinite number of "thank yous" for believing in my voice and this ancient vision to bring more balance and harmony into our world. Thank you, everyone behind the scenes such as Damian, Ashley, Maria and many more at Findhorn Press and Inner Traditions, for carrying amazing visionary ideas out into the world and for giving wings to mine.

Infinite love and gratitude to my wonderfully supportive and patient husband and hero, Mark. You gave me endless love and courage to finally finish one of my many book ideas. Thank you for sharing life, wild adventures, hard work, and your giant, beautiful heart. And thank you for being the brave man who walks beside me and the animals, teaching understanding and compassion.

A big thank you to Dr. Allen Schoen, DVM, for his support, kind words, and his many years spent championing wholistic healing options for animals. You too, are my hero. Thank you to my many mentors of the Five Elements, the brave, fun, and quintessential Fire element Dr. Kerry Ridgeway (in spirit), Dr. Xiu, and Dr. Wong who taught me to "treat the spleen, she is queen!" Thanks to Dave Meyer, the artist of wheels and wood. Sweet hugs and thanks to Susan Tenney for her gifts of acu-wisdom and experience and her deep breadth of knowledge and teaching. Wagging tails and high fives to the master trainer Suzanne Clothier for intimately understanding my need to create more understanding of animal/human relationships.

Many thanks to all my colleagues, clients, friends, and neighbors who have contributed, listened, shared, and cheered me on: Sue, Karen, Lynette, Vicky, Connie, Veronica & Bob, Lucy, Kristy, Sarah, Joy, Elena, Georgia, Mindy, Pam & John, Perry, Peter, Marianne, Debranne, Gina, Don and Michael. You have been the gentle breezes under my wings.

And I give a heart full of gratitude to the many, many, many, animals that have taught me so much about life, healing, humans, ways of being and doing, and love. You have been my family and always will be. Special blessings and gratitude to Cedar, Sage, Louie, Max, Madison, Grizzly, Timber, K.C. Brutus, Sadie, Prince, Wilbur, Luna, Pretzel, Smokey, and a number of cats, other dogs, and horses that have graced my life and home with genuine devotion, inspired teachings, endless love and companionship, and buckets of oxytocin. Infinite gratitude to each of you for sharing your lives with me. You have been my center of gravity.

To all my medicine animals that walk and fly beside me, thank you for guiding me, showing up when I need you, and making my life rich with wonder and grace. Special blessings to a big black Water horse named Connection. You changed my life's pathway and although it took me several years to find it, I now feel the deepest gratitude for your guidance and sacrifice.

And to Mother Nature, our true mother, who teaches us to listen, watch, appreciate, and respect through her wondrous fascinations and live-giving joy. Let's all find ways to protect her benevolence and reciprocity and give back. This planet is our home.

Home is gratitude.
Home is compassion.
Home is empathy.
Home is understanding.
Home is in our hearts.
And so it is.

About the Author

Photo by Mark Johnson

Domestic animals to exotics, wildlife, and nearly everything in between has been in Elizabeth Anne Johnson's hands and has left imprints on her heart. Elizabeth has gathered nearly 40 years of experience in diverse animal-related fields, including canine and equine therapy and rehabilitation on competitive, service, military, police, and companion animals. She has worked as a small/large/exotic animal veterinary technician and instructor and in the wildlife world as a biologist, instructor, and rehabilitator.

She has received incredible gifts of wisdom and science from doctors, veterinarians, and other healers. But by far, her most potent teachers have been the animals themselves, teaching her self-awareness, compassion, empathy, advocacy, and how to truly listen. How to truly heal.

She works from deep clinical understanding, empathy, and compassion to find the "health" of each animal while promoting well-being in the physical, spiritual, and emotional realm of all involved. The owners and caretakers that love and care for their animals have gifted her the understanding of the depth of the human heart, a heart that often knows no boundaries when it comes to loving their animals.

Elizabeth is an author, a TEDx speaker ("Four Life Lessons from Our Old Dogs"), and she contributes blog articles and webinars to numerous rescue organizations.

Last, but by no means least, her own animals have gifted their lives, wisdom, and devotion in return for great care, big chunks of her heart, and some great smells when she gets home each day.

Elizabeth happily lives with her wildlife veterinarian husband and hero, Mark Johnson, on Whidbey Island, Washington. They enjoy hiking, kayaking, gardening, supporting a sustainable community, and howling at night with their rescue dogs Wilbur and Pretzel, the cute girlie dog in the photo.

For more information, visit **www.ElizabethAnneJohnson.com** and **www.4LeggedWellness.com.**

Index

Also of Interest

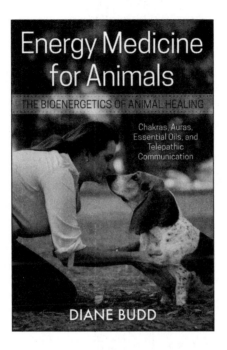

Energy Medicine for Animals

by Diane Budd

A PRACTICAL HANDBOOK on the bioenergetics of animal healing, explaining how to work with the energy fields, auras, and chakras of horses, cats, and dogs. Diane Budd explains how to use high sense perception and illustrates what happens in the energy fields of humans and animals when they connect telepathically. With case studies to showcase the effects of vibrational medicine.

978-1-6205-5840-9

FINDHORN PRESS

Life-Changing Books

Learn more about us and our books at

www.findhornpress.com

For information on the Findhorn Foundation:

www.findhorn.org